Chasing an Elusive God

The Bible's Quest and Ours

Colin

Chasing an Elusive God

The Bible's Quest and Ours

Ray Vincent

Hope it doesn't send you to sleep!

Ray

CHRISTIAN
ALTERNATIVE

Winchester, UK
Washington, USA

First published by Christian Alternative, 2013
Christian Alternative is an imprint of John Hunt Publishing Ltd., Laurel House,
Station Approach, Alresford, Hants, SO24 9JH, UK
office1@jhpbooks.net
www.johnhuntpublishing.com
www.christian-alternative.com

For distributor details and how to order please visit the 'Ordering' section on our website.

Text copyright: Ray Vincent 2012

ISBN: 978 1 84694 714 8

A CIP catalogue record for this book is available from the British Library.

Design: Stuart Davies

Printed and bound by CPI Group (UK) Ltd, Croydon, CR0 4YY

We operate a distinctive and ethical publishing philosophy in all
areas of our business, from our global network of authors to
production and worldwide distribution.

CONTENTS

Notes and Acknowledgements

In the interests of inter-faith respect, I use the expressions BCE (Before the Common Era) and CE (Common Era) in place of the traditional "BC" and "AD".

I have also avoided the term "the Old Testament", preferring to say "the Hebrew scriptures" or "the Jewish scriptures" in recognition of the fact that these writings come to us from the Jews and were already holy scripture before Christianity began. At the same time, I do not hesitate to use the expression "New Testament", because the concept of a "new covenant" is an essential part of Christian faith. This is not a mark of disrespect to the Jewish faith but a matter of respectful theological disagreement.

Bible quotations are generally from the New Revised Standard Version, but I have used the Authorized (King James) Version in places where it is very familiar and well-loved, especially in the psalms.

Some of the Bible stories referred to are told in full, because part of the aim of this book is to encourage people unfamiliar with the Bible to start reading it. Readers who have known these stories since childhood will, I am sure, bear with this and may want to skip the re-telling, though in fact there is no harm in any of us refreshing our memory and sometimes seeing familiar things in a fresh light.

I wish to thank Tim Bulkeley, Robert Draycott, Gordon and Joyce Dykes, Dale Edmondson, John Henson, Barrie Hibbert, Nigel Jones, Michael Taylor, Janet Tollington and Peter West for reading the manuscript at various stages of its development and offering very helpful suggestions. I am also indebted to numerous writers and people with whom I have had conversations, but the responsibility for what this book now contains, and for any unintentional misinformation, is of course my own.

I would welcome feedback through my blog:
http://letthebiblebeitself.blogspot.com

Prologue: The Dream

AT THE beginning of history, human beings began to dream... Their dreams were their fears and their hopes. They dreamed up demons and spirits and hostile gods who caused disease, destruction and death. They dreamed up benevolent spirits who protected them, creative spirits who made the crops grow, happy spirits who made the flowers blossom and inspired people to dance and sing, mysterious spirits who gave them feelings they could not explain.

Then some people became richer and more powerful than others, and they dreamed up gods who protected their wealth and power and kept the poor in their place. They dreamed up national gods who helped them in their battles and defeated other nations. They dreamed up rebel gods who helped them overthrow those more powerful than themselves. They dreamed up power struggles in Heaven reflecting the power struggles on earth, myths to explain why the world is as it is.

*Then someone said: "This can't be right! Let's be logical about it: someone has to be in charge of the whole lot. If there is 'god', there can only be **one** God". And people agreed there could only be one God. But what kind of God?*

So people dreamed up a God who controls everything, creating good and evil, light and darkness, life and death, a God against whom we are all helpless.

But those who were oppressed and abused said: "This can't go on forever!" And they dreamed up a God of justice who favours the good and doesn't allow the wicked to get away with it. And in the name of this God of justice the poor and the weak felt free, and sang songs of hope.

But then the powerful took this God over, and changed the dream to a God of laws and rules, who punishes the little weaknesses of the poor and threatens them with Hell, but overlooks the violence of the powerful because it is "necessary" to keep society in order.

And then someone who was in love said: "Love is the greatest thing

I

in the world. If God is the greatest, God must be loving". So people dreamed up a God who loves and cares and wants to be our friend. A God like that would not want war and violence, nor punishment, nor barriers of race and class. Such a God would want us all to love one another.

This was not a very popular idea. People who preached about such a God were sometimes scorned as impractical dreamers. Even worse, they were set up on a pedestal and worshipped, and their teaching was twisted so that once again it served the purposes of the powerful.

Time passed, and circumstances changed. Hindus dreamed of one God in many manifestations. Buddhists dreamed of an eternal Spirit, forming and re-forming itself in every living creature. Jews in all their suffering dreamed of a God whose justice is slow and hard to see, yet perfect. Christians dreamed of a God who came down to earth and became one with suffering humanity. Muslims dreamed of a God who is merciful and compassionate, whom to obey is peace. Sikhs dreamed of a God in whose eyes all faiths are equal.

And then women began to say: "Why do the men assume God is male?" And they dreamed up a God who is our Mother, warm and loving, but strong and fierce to protect us.

And black people, setting themselves free from centuries of oppression, said: "Black is beautiful. God is beautiful. God is black".

And then gay people said: "Why do all the God-dreamers condemn us? God made us too. He made us different, because he loves variety".

And so we go on, generation after generation, whoever we are, arguing and praying, in our hopes and in our fears dreaming up the God we need.

And that is how men and women said: "Let us create God in our image".

BUT perhaps there is another story...

From eternity God has had dreams. God's dreams are energy, forming matter. God dreamed up a universe, with billions of galaxies full of stars. And because God dreamed it, it was real. And God's dreaming made planets, and life, evolving in thousands of shapes and colours, and intelligence, and human beings.

And God, surprised and delighted at God's own creativity, said: "They are so beautiful! I can see myself in them!"

And then God said: "I won't tell them I made them. I'll let them dream me up. I'll let them argue about me. They may learn more about me that way. And who knows? I may even learn something more about myself."

Introduction

The conviction behind the writing of this book is that *the Bible is worth reading*. Far from being a dull tome we ought to read just because it is "holy", it is in fact a fascinating collection of literature, full of thrilling and amusing stories, beautiful and moving poetry, and a rich vein of real humanity.

This view of the Bible runs contrary to the perception of many in our present-day Western culture. I still remember a little poem from a college magazine of the 1950s, though unfortunately I cannot recall the name of the author. It is written in the condensed, alliterative form of a Welsh *englyn* (the "dd" in "Rhondda" is pronounced like the "th" in "thou"):

"A black scroll on the bleak scree: a language
that's written in many;
O weary mine of words to me,
thou bitter Rhondda beauty"

This verse encapsulates something of the South Wales valleys in the 50s with their bleak environment and their culture dominated by mining and the Bible. At the same time it expresses the feeling of many people today who feel the Bible as a burden, an oppression from which they are glad to have escaped. Wales has its own particular history in this respect, but these ambivalent feelings can be found in other places too.

The Bible is an integral part of our Western cultural heritage. Whenever we say things like "a law unto itself", "the salt of the earth", "O ye of little faith", "all things to all men", or "the powers that be", we are quoting from the Authorized, or King James, Version of the Bible, David Crystal[1] estimates that there are 257 idioms in present-day English that derive from it. It truly is "a language that's written in many".

The Bible is still embedded in our culture. In law courts people hold the Bible in their hand as they swear to tell "the truth, the whole truth, and nothing but the truth". Incoming Presidents of the United States take their oath of office on the Bible. On the popular British radio programme, *Desert Island Discs*, when famous people are asked what they would like to have with them to read on the imaginary desert island, they are told they will in any case be provided with the two big books that are regarded as the staple fare of English reading, namely the Bible and the complete works of Shakespeare; though recently a few of those participating have broken tradition by saying they would not want a Bible.

In most ordinary homes there is more likely to be a Bible than a copy of the complete works of Shakespeare, but it is probably even less likely to be opened and read. Present-day Western culture is rapidly forgetting the Bible. It is interesting to note in radio and television quiz programs that people who have an enormous store of knowledge about history, literature, music and even classical mythology nearly always fail to answer the most elementary questions about Bible stories. This is not only true of people who are not "religious". Regular churchgoers too are much more ignorant of the Bible than previous generations were. Many never pick up a Bible to read it, and their only exposure to it is the reading of the lesson in church on Sunday, to which they are often not very attentive. Some have a guilty feeling about this, but whenever they make a resolution to start reading the Bible it somehow seems a tedious and daunting task.

Much of the reason for this lies in the associations and memories that surround it. In Britain it is associated with things like compulsory school assembly and church parade. Experience of it in adult life is mostly confined to weddings, funerals and carol services. In those contexts the reading of the "lesson" is a ritual, often done in a solemn and artificial tone. A passage is read with no introduction of its background, and usually from the King James Version, a translation that for all its elegance of style is hardly accessible to most people today, having been made in 1611 in language that was slightly old-fashioned even then. Add to this the fact that in many ethical controversies those who most readily quote the Bible seem always to represent the more conservative and judgmental point of view, and it is not surprising that the Bible is not popular.

Of course we cannot pretend that the Bible is "up to date". It comes to us from a culture that is in many ways alien to our own. This means that while we can sometimes recognize in it the passions and aspirations of human beings just like ourselves, there are other times when we cannot understand what it is talking about or feel any sympathy for its attitudes. We need to be honest about this, because this kind of honest reaction is the beginning of real appreciation.

We have to recognize the Bible's multiple human origins. Though for many centuries it has been seen as one holy book, and the way Bibles are printed usually conveys that impression, it is in fact a collection of different kinds of literature written (or spoken) by many different people spread over a time span of more than a thousand years. No-one would think of producing an anthology of English literature from Beowulf to the latest twenty-first century short story in which everything was printed in the same style, in double columns, with every sentence numbered, no introductions and no distinction between prose and poetry. But this is something like what we have in the Bible.

It is of course divided into books (sixty-six if you are a Protestant, more if you are Roman Catholic or Eastern Orthodox), and most people know that these books were written by different people. However, the real picture is more complex than that. Very few of these books were "written" in the sense that modern books are written. They were compiled from individual sayings, poems and stories that had often been repeated for generations by word of mouth. The compiling of them was a gradual process that often had within it an element of adaptation and alteration, and happened in the thick of religious and political controversy. We shall see in Chapter 2 how modern scholarship has made us more aware of this process and made the Bible much more exciting by enabling us to see into the turbulent world out of which it was created.

The Bible is a human creation, and all the more wonderful for that. We need a re-think about the Bible similar to the re-think many believers have had about creation. Many of us now find that a God who has brought the entire universe into being over billions of years and continues to create all the variety of living things through a process of evolution is much more awe-inspiring than one who made everything in six days a few thousand years ago. In the same way, we need to learn that a God whose ways are revealed through the insights, the experiences, the arguments and even the conflicts of human beings is much more real than one who has spoken in a monologue from Heaven and put it all down in a book.

The Bible is not a book of answers but a book of questions. Its writers, like ourselves, were seekers. They were trying to make sense of life and the world. They were telling the story of their spiritual experience, interpreting it in different ways, and at the same time trying to cope with the down-to-earth realities of pain, bereavement, hardship and conflict. We appreciate the Bible best by entering into their experience and joining in the ongoing conversation. Sometimes we can recognize our own quest in that of the Bible writers. At other times it looks as if we today are not asking the same questions, or if we are asking them, not coming to the same answers. But even this makes the Bible no less worth reading, because it confronts us with a different way of thinking and prompts us to stop and explore how our own contemporary spiritual quest relates to that of the Bible.

I hope this book will stimulate the reader to open the Bible, find fresh enjoyment in reading it, and come to love it "warts and all". I hope too that some of the information it gives will be a helpful guide for *dipping into* the Bible. The Bible is a very long and complex book, and most people who set out to read it from beginning to end tend to break their resolution about halfway through the Book of Exodus, if not sooner. Dipping into it as one dips into an anthology of poetry is a much better way of appreciating it. With a little understanding of the historical background and of the types of literature that make up the Bible, it is possible at virtually any place in it to recognize what one is reading and feel something of the concern and passion behind it. The Bible then becomes "three dimensional", not just a flat collection of holy texts but a window into a whole world.

Notes

1. David Crystal, *Begat: The King James Bible and the English Language* (OUP 2010), p 258

I

Never Mind the Authority: Feel the Power!

"Do not seek to follow in the footsteps of the wise. Seek what they sought"
(Matsuo Basho, seventeenth century Japanese poet)

Much talk about the Bible is bogged down by an obsession with authority. At one extreme we have the conservative believers who say that the entire Bible "from cover to cover" is the infallible Word of God. We sometimes call them "literalists", but this is not quite true, because no one actually takes *everything* in the Bible literally. Even the most extreme fundamentalists realise as much as anyone else that when God is called a Shepherd or a Rock, or when he is said to "make bare his holy arm" (Is 52:10) these are metaphorical expressions. Most conservative Bible believers recognize too that the parables of Jesus were stories he created to make a point rather than historical accounts of actual people. However, their general tendency is always to take the Bible literally unless there is an obvious case for not doing so. If a passage looks like history, from their point of view it is history. Whatever the Bible says about the nature of God they take as a fact, and when the Bible gives moral instructions they believe we have to obey them as coming from God himself.

At the other extreme are those who say that the Bible is a load of myths, fairy tales, propaganda and primitive taboos, and is therefore not worth reading. The one thing these extremes have in common is an assumption that the value of the Bible depends purely on its factual accuracy, a strange assumption when you think about it. No-one expects us to believe that the works of Shakespeare are infallible, but on the other hand no-one suggests they are a waste of time because the "historical" plays are inaccurate and biased, and the others are all fiction!

Between the two extremes are the endless discussions among theologians, biblical scholars and ordinary people in church discussion groups as to what is meant by "the authority of the Bible". Yes, they say, the Bible is the Word of God, and it is the authority (the "supreme" authority, most would say) for Christian faith and practice. However, they add, we have to be careful how we use it. We have to check different translations, or look up commentaries, in case of misunderstanding. We have to see each passage within its context, learn something about the background, try to recognize what the writer really intended to say, take cultural differences into account, and so on and so on, but it is still the authority. Here the idea of the Bible as the author-itative word of God often seems to suffer "death by a thousand qualifications". There is also behind all this a kind of lurking fundamentalism, an assumption that once we have removed all possibilities of misunderstanding we shall find what the Bible *really* says, and at that point we shall have no choice but to submit to its authority.

Why "Authority"?

All this assumes that the point of the Bible, the only reason why we should read it at all, is its authority. But why should this necessarily be so? We do not make that assumption about all books. Of course we expect school text books to be factually reliable. We recognize that the constitution of a state is binding on its government and citizens, and that a game can be very confusing and frustrating if all the players do not respect the authority of the rule book. But this represents only a small fraction of the literature in existence: we do not have the same expectation of everything we read.

Many of the people who contributed to the Bible did in fact claim to be speaking with authority. Some of them were legis-lators. Some were priests and teachers. Some were prophets

declaring with absolute conviction the message they believed
God had revealed to them. They often prefaced their words with
"Thus says the LORD...". Most of the Bible writers talk of God as
someone of whose existence and nature they are quite sure. But
this is only one side of the Bible's nature. Even those who claim
to be speaking with authority often contradict one another. The
"true" prophets and the "false" prophets stood in opposition to
each other, and only time could reveal who was right. Jesus
spoke "as one having authority" (Matt 7:28), but so in a sense did
his opponents who saw themselves as the authoritative interpreters of the divine Law.

There is in fact an ongoing debate throughout the Bible about
God's nature and ways. Does God visit the sins of the fathers on
the children and grandchildren? It depends whether you read
Exodus 20 or Ezekiel 18. Was the monarchy in Israel ordained
and anointed by God, or was it the result of the people's loss of
faith that God would always provide the right leaders at the
right time? It depends whether you read Psalm 2 or 1 Samuel 8.
Is there any place for Gentiles in God's holy people? It depends
whether you read Ezra or Ruth. Religious people, especially
those in the Abrahamic faiths of Judaism, Christianity and Islam,
have always argued with each other. The argument begins in the
Bible itself.

There are several reasons why we perhaps ought to avoid
using the word "authority" in connection with the Bible. For
many of us today, faith is not something laid down from the
beginning but an ongoing spiritual quest, a search for meaning.
This makes it in some ways analogous to the scientific search for
truth. Scientists do not talk of "authority" in the sense of
something fixed and unchangeable. Science is all about investi-
gating, questioning and experimenting. A theory is accepted and
used as long as it works, but if difficulties or anomalies arise it
needs to be tested again and eventually replaced by a new theory
that accounts for the facts in a more complete and satisfactory

way. We can in fact see this kind of process going on within the Bible. The Book of Job questions the theory that goodness is rewarded with prosperity and sin punished with misfortune, the "master theory" behind the books of Judges, Samuel and Kings. The Book of Ecclesiastes challenges the "theory" that lies behind most of the rest of the Bible, and questions whether life has any meaning at all.

Our perspective on the world has changed in the past few centuries. We can no longer be unaware of the immense variety of human experience and spirituality that exists in the world. Many people in the West today are looking away from the religious tradition in which they grew up and exploring the wisdom to be found in cultures that have developed separately from the Judaeo-Christian one. Buddhism is popular in Western countries. Meditative and therapeutic traditions such as yoga, Reiki and so on are widely practised, sometimes with an element of the religious cultures from which they came, but sometimes dissociated from any particular religion. "Gurus" like Maharishi Mahesh Yogi, Bhagwan Shree Rajneesh, Krishnamurti and others have been influential in many people's thinking. The Hari Krishna people in their saffron robes have become a familiar sight in some Western cities. There is widespread interest in indigenous traditions like those of the Native Americans or the Australian aborigines, and the pre-Christian traditions in Europe, like Wicca and paganism. It has become much more difficult to claim that ultimate and complete truth is only found in the particular tradition that European culture has inherited from the scriptures of one small nation living on the east coast of the Mediterranean.

Even more challenging is what we now know about the vastness of the universe and the billions of years of its history. Is it any longer reasonable to believe that the Creator, the incomprehensible energy and intelligence behind the whole universe, has fully and finally revealed Himself (even if we can still use that personal, masculine expression) in a set of writings produced by people living in one small corner of this one planet in little more than a thousand years of its history? And when we look at this set of writings with all its inconsistencies, untidiness and ethically mixed content, the idea becomes even less likely.

In modern Western culture we have developed insights into human personality and society that have taught us to be wary of the whole concept of "authority". Authority is a human construct, usually veiling the desire of some people to have power over others. It goes against today's ideas about democracy. The assumption in most countries today is that our rulers govern us not because they are inherently superior to us but because we, by voting for them, have delegated to them the power to make decisions on our behalf. If we are unhappy with the way they govern, we reserve the right to replace them with others. Whatever "authority" they have is what we have given them. Not only in politics but in most areas of life, we do not generally accept rules if we can see no clear reason for them. "Authority" is often something people fall back on when their arguments are weak: "Never mind why, do this because I say so and I'm the boss". In the religious sphere the notion of authority enables churches to control their members by keeping them in fear of being condemned and excluded as "heretics", or even of going to Hell. It is basically a legal and political rather than a spiritual concept.

The Bible as Art

To deny the "authority" of the Bible in this way is not for a moment to deny its value or its power. I once went to the National Gallery in London with an elderly friend who was a very talented amateur painter. Seeing Van Gogh's *Sunflowers* for the first time, she was not impressed at all. Her reaction was "*I could paint sunflowers better than that!*" In a sense she was right. She could have made a much more *accurate* picture of a vase of sunflowers. No doubt Van Gogh could have done so too if he had wanted to, but that was not his intention. Van Gogh did not set out to inform us what sunflowers look like: a photograph or a botanical drawing could tell us that. What he did was to contemplate sunflowers, to open his heart to them, and to express in his painting the feeling they gave him. Because he did this we can look at that picture today, feel something of what he felt and see sunflowers, and perhaps the whole world, in a new way. That is what great art is about.

To talk of the "authority" of a work of art in the way we usually talk of the "authority" of the Bible would be meaningless. A work of art may say something very important to us. It may in the long run influence our character and make a difference to the way we live. It may make us more appreciative of beauty, more aware of the tragedy of life, more understanding and compassionate. But it does not give us straightforward information or tell us what to do. A work of art is hardly ever called "authoritative", but is often described as "powerful", "provocative" or "challenging".

The Bible too can be appreciated in this way. The American writer Ernest Sutherland Bates produced in the 1930s a book called *The Bible Designed to be Read as Literature*[1], a selection of excerpts from the King James Bible chosen for their lasting literary value irrespective of the belief or unbelief of the reader. Though it achieved some popularity, it did not appeal to the majority of Christian believers. The more orthodox would be offended by the very idea of editing out the "inferior" parts of the Bible and retaining only those the editor approved of, but for many others too it would not seem appropriate to present the Bible as a kind of coffee-table book to be calmly enjoyed by the connoisseur of literature.

For anyone who takes spirituality seriously a religious writing cannot simply entertain us or satisfy our historical curiosity. We have to engage seriously with it because it deals with the fundamental questions of life. For those of us whose beliefs and attitudes are shaped by the Judaeo-Christian tradition, the people who produced the Bible are our ancestors in faith and spiritual exploration. Their search for God is our search too. However elegant the archaic English of the King James Bible may be, believers do not see literary style as the main point of the Bible.

However, we have to beware here of a false dichotomy. No work of art can be properly appreciated just on an aesthetic level, or judged simply in terms of its appeal to the eyes or the ears, or the craftsmanship of its design. To appreciate any work of art properly we have to open our minds and our hearts to it: we have to let it grip us. Art that is merely "pleasant" or "pretty" is not the greatest art. Great art is challenging. Rather than soothing us, it can make us uncomfortable. To talk of the Bible as a work of art, therefore, is not for a moment to deny its power to challenge us. Indeed, even for those who are convinced that the Bible has an important message for people today, the best way of hearing that message is probably not by reading it as a book of authoritative information and instruction. We should rather allow it to be fully itself, entering into all its moods and really listening to the voices of all its writers.

The Bible speaks with many voices, voices that often disagree with each other. In a sense the only "authority" it can be said to have is the authority of people being themselves, speaking from their own conviction and honestly relating their own experience. Today, in a culture that challenges all settled forms of authority, we can see in the Bible itself how truth can emerge through the variety of human experience and human points of view. The Bible does not tell us directly about God: it records the experiences and the thoughts of people who in different ways were searching for God, or who believed they had met God, and it invites us to join in their conversation.

The writers of some parts of the Bible, like Job, Ecclesiastes,

Jonah and some of the psalms, were consciously engaged in a quest rather than making authoritative pronouncements. They asked questions that were unanswerable, but still wrestled for an answer. Today's readers may well warm to these writings more than to other parts of the Bible. At the same time this may help us to see even the more dogmatic parts in a different light. Looking beneath the surface, and appreciating the passions behind them, we may come to see that they too, in their way, are part of a search rather than a solution.

It is my hope that this book will help readers to see the Bible not as the kind of "authority" that puts the damper on any new, adventurous thinking, but as part of the ongoing human search for truth, for understanding, and for God.

Notes

1. This seems to have first appeared in 1936, and was followed by a number of editions, some called *The Bible: Designed to be Read as Living Literature*. The latest seems to be that by Wick Allison, published by Simon and Schuster in 1993.

2

The Bible as a Human Creation

Our ability to see the Bible "in three dimensions" has been hugely enhanced by the work of biblical critics, the scholars who have been studying it scientifically for the past two hundred years or so. They have given us new insights into its meaning and its background. In the process they have cast doubt on many things that were once taken for granted, like the accuracy of the history, the authorship of the books and so on. At the same time they have opened our eyes to the living world out of which the biblical writings came.

Textual critics have sifted through the manuscripts and brought us a Bible that is nearer to the original. Literary critics have examined the form and style of the biblical writings and brought us a clearer picture of how they were put together, where they originated, and how they were used in the life of ancient Israel or of the Jewish and early Christian communities. Archaeological investigation of sites mentioned in the Bible, and the study of ancient inscriptions and documents, have thrown fascinating light on the history behind the stories. Some conservative Christians have laid great stress on the way in which archaeology "proves" that the Bible is true, but this is only one side of the story. Some archaeological discoveries have indeed confirmed biblical accounts: it would be strange if they did not. Others, however, have cast considerable doubt on them. Anthropologists have cast light on the meaning of many customs, ceremonies and ways of life that are mentioned in the Bible. Social studies have investigated the form of society in biblical times. For those who are willing to leave fundamentalism behind, all this has made the Bible a much more interesting and exciting book to read.

However, *there is one big drawback*. The more we read about the findings of the biblical scholars, the more we ordinary readers become aware of our ignorance. To keep up to date with the latest discoveries and theories is difficult for the scholars themselves: like all academics these days, they tend to specialise in ever smaller areas. It is even more difficult for the busy preacher who learned some of the results of scholarship while in training but now finds it hard to keep up with developments. What chance has the lay person who works in a secular job and struggles to find time even to *read* the Bible? It is little wonder that many people who are very intelligent and competent in their own field tend to fall back on naïve fundamentalism when it comes to the Bible. They are quite content to take it all at face value and assume that the writers were just writing down the facts: it makes life so much simpler. Some people realise that this is wrong, but feel unqualified to practise the alternative. While being ready and willing to accept the findings of critical scholarship, they are hampered simply by ignorance. Is there a middle way, a way of reading the Bible realistically and critically, but without getting caught up in the treadmill of feeling that we have to keep up to date with the latest theory of the scholars?

Do It Yourself!

Part of the answer to this is that the historical-critical method is not quite as daunting as we sometimes think. Biblical scholarship, both ancient and modern, has always started with someone reading the Bible, being puzzled about something, and looking for an answer. Every one of us can start at the same place. It is impossible to be right about everything, and it is not necessary. What is needed is a curious, critical *attitude* that gets us into the habit of "reading between the lines".

I learned many things about the Bible when studying for my degree in theology. Many of them I retained in my memory just long enough to write an essay or pass an exam. Some I remember to this day, but by now (like the commentaries I bought with my student grant) they are more than half a century out of date. But the most important thing I learned in studying for that degree was an *approach*, a way of looking at the Bible. Having been in the habit of reading the Bible since childhood and generally accepting what it said, or rather what I had been *taught* it said, I had to learn to look at it in a different way and ask different questions.

It is this *way of reading*, rather than any specific facts or theories, that is crucial, and the main features of it can be learned fairly easily by anyone who is willing to make the mental jump. It is a matter of taking off the spectacles of a religious upbringing (or for some people the spectacles of their reaction against religion) and trying to read the Bible afresh. It is giving up the assumption that it says what we were taught it says, and the expectation that every bit of it will fit in with our understanding of "Christian doctrine". It means remembering that the books of the Bible were not written as a direct message from God to the twenty-first century, but by different people for different purposes at different times. It means learning to ask not "what is the correct way of interpreting this passage?", but "what was this writer trying to say?"

We can then start noticing the details: the inconsistencies, the different versions of the same story, the "seams" where different bits seem to have been stitched together. We can notice odd expressions and start thinking about how they may have got there. Once you get into the habit of doing this, which after all is where all critical scholarship started, it is surprising how much you can discover just by using your common sense.

We can begin this approach at the very beginning of the Bible, with the story of creation, or rather the stories of creation, because there are two.

The first chapter of Genesis is an elegantly arranged, majestically written story of how God, just by speaking the word, created "the heavens and the earth" and everything in them, and saw that it was all good. It is tragic that so much attention is given to arguing about "creation *versus* evolution" that we often fail to notice what a magnificent piece of writing this passage is. If we look at the story carefully we will find details in it that are very interesting and at first sight puzzling. For instance, why does it say that God made "the two great lights", one for the day and one for the night (Gen 1:16)? The writer is obviously talking about the sun and the moon, so why does he not say so? It is as if he is carefully avoiding using the words. Why would he do that? Has it perhaps something to do with the fact that most ancient cultures worshipped the sun and the moon as gods? Our own pagan heritage is still with us in the names "Sunday" and "Monday".

This story reaches its conclusion in verse 3 of chapter 2. There is then a formal statement, "These are the generations of the heavens and the earth, when they were created", and a new story begins halfway through verse 4. The original biblical writings were not divided into chapters and verses: the verse divisions in fact date only as far back as the sixteenth century. At this point the division for some reason seems to be particularly inappropriate.

The new story begins: "In the day that the LORD God made the earth and the heavens". Here there is already an inconsistency: not "the week" but "the day". There is also obvious contradiction in the order of creation. In chapter 1 the plants are made first, then the sea creatures and the birds, then the land animals, and finally human beings, an order quite similar to that of evolution as we now understand it. In chapter 2 it is specifically stated that God made a man before there were any plants in the earth. The order of creation was first man, then plants, then animals, and finally woman!

Moreover, the Creator is now not "God", but "the LORD God". The word "LORD" printed in block capitals in English Bibles refers to the proper name of God as worshipped by Jews. The Hebrew scriptures were originally written with consonants only, and the name of God was YHWH, which when turned from Hebrew into Latin script becomes JHVH. Because the name is so sacred, Jews for many centuries have been reluctant to say it aloud, and the custom developed of saying "the Lord" instead. When vowel signs were added to the text to assist the reader, JHVH was given the vowels of the word that meant "the Lord", in order to remind the reader what to say. The English translators followed the letters as they stood, producing "Jehovah", a hybrid name with the consonants of one word and the vowels of another! The King James Version and other English Bibles follow the Jewish tradition, usually rendering the name as "the LORD" in block capitals. The Jerusalem Bible is the only major version that uses what scholars believe was the original name, "Yahweh".

Although YHWH came to be too sacred even to mention, it seems that in this creation story, as in many other stories in the early part of the Bible, it is simply the name of a powerful but rather human-like being. He is a "hands on" creator. He "formed man from the dust of the ground, and breathed into his nostrils the breath of life". Then he "planted" a garden. Concerned that the man was lonely, he made the animals and "brought" them to Adam. None of them cured his loneliness, so he put Adam to sleep and "took one of his ribs and closed up the place with flesh", then made that rib into a woman. Later we find him "walking in the garden at the time of the evening breeze". Even after Adam and Eve had disobeyed, he "made garments of skins" for them and "clothed them" because they were embarrassed by their nakedness. So different from the cosmic Creator of the first chapter who just issues orders from Heaven!

This homely story continues into chapter 3. Here it is particularly important to forget what we have been taught about the story and simply read it as it is. In Christian theology it is seen as the story of "the fall", that major cosmic disaster by which humanity was estranged from God and plunged into "original sin" (or even according to some theologians "total depravity") and creation itself was cursed with mortality. However, if we read it just as it is we can see that none of this is said in the story itself. It seems to be the Apostle Paul who first interpreted it in that way, but it is questionable whether even he meant what some Christian theologians have made of it.

What is this story really about? It looks as if it is not so much about divine commands and human sin as about the peculiar nature of human beings: curious, questioning, rebellious, enjoying nakedness and yet embarrassed by it, living with pain and hard work and longing for a paradise they feel they once had; possessing immense, godlike knowledge, and yet destined to die and rot in the ground just like the other animals. It is a very perceptive picture of the human predicament. Nothing is said here about humanity becoming totally estranged from God or inherently "sinful". Adam and Eve are simply turned out of the garden where conditions were relatively easy and made to wrest a living from difficult ground and live a life of toil and pain because now they "know too much". It sounds very much like growing up and facing the real world, and perhaps that is partly what the story was meant to convey.

This story has all the marks of a simple folk tale, a myth about human life, revolving around personalities rather than cosmology. As such, it sounds much older, more "primitive", than the story in the first chapter. At the same time, it is easy to see why the story that came later in time was put first when Genesis was put together in its present form. It obviously seemed a more fitting opening to a grand epic about the beginnings of the world. And yet both of them in their different ways are an attempt to explain the inexplicable mystery of where this world came from and how it came to be as it is.

The fact that these two very different stories are juxtaposed at the beginning is also significant when we stop to think about it. Though the first five books of the Bible are traditionally called the Books of Moses, these inconsistencies and different styles suggest

22

that they could not have been written by one author. In the final form in which we now have them they are obviously the work of an editor or compiler rather than a writer. This editor, or team of editors, was putting together stories that already existed. It is also evident that they never thought of asking the question "which story is true?" Both stories were old, so they each had an honoured place in the collection. This is a feature we find very frequently throughout the Bible once we start looking for it. It suggests very strongly that the writers of the Bible were not nearly as concerned about the literal truth of stories as many of its modern readers are.

In the New Testament, the Gospels are a rich field for the curious reader looking for the "seams". There are four different versions of the story of Jesus. The Gospel of John is very different in style and content from the others, but Matthew, Mark and Luke have many stories and sayings in common, and are often almost word for word the same. It is very interesting to compare a story or a saying as it is given in the different Gospels. This can be done either by having several Bibles open in front of you, or by using bookmarks to flick to and fro between the Gospels. I once did this with a Sunday school class of eleven year olds. They were fascinated, and so was I, because they were pointing out things I had not thought of myself!

This great similarity of the Gospels already raises a question. Did the writer of one Gospel copy from another? And if so, which version is the original and which is the copy? When we look at the differences, it usually looks as if Mark was the first and it was Matthew and Luke who copied Mark and made some alterations and additions. But why would Matthew, who was one of the Twelve and presumably an eye-witness to most if not all of the events, need to copy from a written account by Mark, who was not one of the Twelve? This leads us to start questioning whether Matthew the apostle was actually the author of the Gospel. In fact, we may question whether Matthew was one of the Twelve at all. It is only in the Gospel of Matthew that he has that name: in the others the tax-collector Jesus called to follow him is called Levi (compare Matt 9:9 with Mark 2:14 and Luke 5:27). The scholars have explanations for these facts, but even today there are disagreements, so there is no point in us ordinary readers worrying too much about getting it right. The main point is that by noticing the similarities and the differences, and thinking about them for ourselves, we can often have interesting insights into the early Christian church as a living community with its own priorities, problems and disagreements.

To take one small example: Mark tells the story of when Jesus went to his home town of Nazareth and the people there treated him rather dismissively because they had known him since he was a boy. Mark concludes the story by saying: "And he could do no deed of power there, except that he laid hands on a few sick people and cured them. And he was amazed at their unbelief" (Mark 6:5-6).

Matthew tells the same story in almost the same words, but he ends it with: "And he did not do many deeds of power there, because of their unbelief" (Matt 13:58). It looks as if Matthew was not happy with Mark's interpretation of the incident. He did not like the idea that the power of Jesus to do miracles could somehow be limited. Nor did he like the idea that Jesus, who was divine and presumably knew everything, could be "amazed". And so he concluded that Jesus *chose* not to do many miracles there, as a way of rebuking them for their unbelief. This little difference in the telling of a story raises a very profound question about the very nature of Jesus. Are we with Mark or Matthew? Do we believe that Jesus' power was limited, or perhaps his confidence wounded, by the experience in Nazareth? But on the other hand are we happy with the idea that Jesus would *choose* not to heal people? And so we find that simply by comparing versions of the same story we are being drawn into the kind of discussions and arguments that occupied the New Testament writers themselves.

Who Wrote the Books?

In the King James Bible and some modern translations the first book is entitled "The First Book of Moses, called Genesis", and there follow the other four "books of Moses": Exodus, Leviticus, Numbers and Deuteronomy. However, as we have already seen from the creation stories, these books show signs of being a compilation of material from different and sometimes contradictory sources, making it very difficult to believe that Moses wrote them all – not to mention the account of his own death in the last chapter of Deuteronomy. The "Book of Moses" titles are omitted in most modern translations, because the actual Hebrew manuscripts do not include a title: the title comes from Jewish tradition. Because of the story of God giving the Commandments to Moses on Mount Sinai, the whole Torah, or Law, that was the heart of the Jewish religion was assumed to have been imparted through Moses. And so, since laws make up a large part of those five books, they came to be seen as the Law (Torah) and attributed in their entirety to Moses.

Similarly, many people think of David as the author of the Book of Psalms. Many of the psalms have a title "A Psalm of David". Unlike the "Book of Moses" titles, these are actually in the Bible manuscripts and not just tradition. However, "A Psalm of David" does not necessarily imply a claim that David is the author. In the Jerusalem Temple the king played a leading role in many of the ceremonies and rituals, so "a Psalm of David" might simply have meant a psalm with royal connections, with "David" being a general title for the king, as was "Caesar" for the Roman Emperor in later times. It is also worth noting that many of the psalms have other titles such as "Of the Korahites" or "A Psalm of Asaph", and some have no title at all. Some of the psalms show clear signs of being written long after the time of David, when his descendants still reigned in Jerusalem, and even later when the Jews were scattered among the nations and hoping to return to their own country. However, David was remembered as a skilful musician (see 1 Sam 16:14-23), and so he came to mean for psalmody what Moses meant for law.

The other great reputed biblical author is King Solomon, thought of as the writer of Proverbs, Ecclesiastes, the Song of Solomon and the book called the Wisdom of Solomon, one of the books known to Protestants as the Apocrypha. It was Solomon's reputation for wisdom that encouraged these ascriptions. Early in the account of his reign there is a story (1 Kgs 3:3-15) of how God appeared to him in a dream and invited him to ask for a gift. Aware of the huge responsibility of the kingdom, he asked for wisdom. His wish was granted, and because he had shown a right sense of priorities God also blessed him with wealth and power. And so the name of Solomon was inseparably associated with wise sayings and writings.

Parts of the Book of Proverbs are ascribed to "Solomon son of David, king of Israel", but there are other parts that are simply called "the words of the wise" (22:17) or "sayings of the wise" (24:23), and at the end of the book are two sections specifically attributed to other people: Agur son of Jakeh (30:1) and King Lemuel (31:1), who is said to be passing on the teachings of his mother. In Ecclesiastes the name of Solomon is not mentioned, but the book is introduced as "The words of the teacher, the son of David, king in Jerusalem". Again, "son" could be a poetic expression for "descendant", as when Jesus is called the "Son of David". The next book is entitled "The Song of Songs, which is Solomon's". Solomon is mentioned several times in it, but not in a way that suggests he is the author (Song 1:5; 3:6-11; 8:11-12). However, the fact of his being mentioned and the saying (1 Kgs 4:32) that Solomon wrote a thousand and five songs probably accounts for the ascription. Another factor could have been that Solomon, who is reputed to have had seven hundred wives and three hundred concubines (1 Kgs 11:3), seemed a likely author for a book of erotic poetry!

We have to remember that the production of literature was

very different in the culture of biblical times from what it is today. Generally, the people who wrote the Bible were not writing books with a view to expressing their individuality or saying something original. They were simply doing a job that was expected of them within the community to which they belonged. Most of the writings in the Bible are anonymous. The writers were also quite happy to honour some eminent teacher by continuing in the spirit of what they believed he taught, either by adding to his works or even by producing whole new books in his name. Often they believed that the revered prophet or wise man or woman of the past was inspiring them as they wrote. This principle is explicit in John's Gospel, where Jesus is represented as saying to his disciples: "I still have many things to say to you, but you cannot bear them now. When the Spirit of truth comes, he will guide you into all the truth... he will take what is mine and declare it to you" (John 16:12-14). This explains why John's Gospel includes so many sayings that are difficult to imagine on the lips of the Jesus portrayed in the other Gospels: the writer believed that he was being inspired to be the mouthpiece of Jesus. In the same way in the Hebrew scriptures, laws continued to be made in the name of Moses, psalms written in the name of David and "words of wisdom" in the name of Solomon.

A clear example of multiple authorship is the Book of Isaiah. This book introduces itself as "The vision of Isaiah son of Amoz, which he saw concerning Judah and Jerusalem in the days of Uzziah, Jotham, Ahaz and Hezekiah, kings of Judah". This places the prophet in the period between about 740 and 700 BCE. It was a period in which the Assyrian Empire was taking over the northern kingdom of Israel (Samaria) and attempting to take over the southern kingdom of Judah as well. Isaiah, living in Jerusalem and being in close contact with the royal court, encouraged the king at the time not to enter into any foolish alliances but to hold on in the faith that God would protect Jerusalem. Chapters 36-39 correspond almost word for word with the history related in 2 Kings 18-20 about how an Assyrian attack on Jerusalem was averted, and relating the part Isaiah played in the crisis.

However, from the beginning of chapter 40 ("Comfort, O comfort my people, says your God...") we seem to be in a totally different situation. The Jews are now exiles in Babylon and there is hope of their return to Judah. Babylon is doomed (Is 47) and its Persian conqueror Cyrus is actually mentioned by name (Is 44:28; 45:1). The fall of Babylon to the Persians took place about 539 BCE, about a hundred and sixty years after the end of Isaiah's career as a prophet. Unless we subscribe to a "magical" idea of prophecy as accurate prediction of events in the remote future, even to the naming of names, we have to conclude that these chapters are the work of a later writer. Their addition to the original Book of Isaiah may have been a matter of economy: papyrus and ink were expensive, and the prophecies of Isaiah were not long enough to fill a whole scroll. The books of Jeremiah and Ezekiel are about the same length as Isaiah, and twelve of what we call the "minor prophets" were actually written on one scroll of similar length.

However, there is a thematic connection between the different parts of Isaiah. They both concern good news for Jerusalem. In the intervening time between Isaiah 39 and 40 Jerusalem had been destroyed by the Babylonians and many of its people taken to Babylon as prisoners. Jeremiah had seen this as an inevitable judgment on the nation's sins and attacked the complacency of those who, perhaps harking back to Isaiah's prophecies, assumed that Jerusalem was indestructible. But now, after fifty years of exile, the new king Cyrus was sending Jews back to live in their own country and re-build Jerusalem. A prophet whose name we do not know saw God at work in this and rejoiced ecstatically over it. It seemed that Isaiah's assurances about God's care for Jerusalem were true after all. This prophet was Isaiah for a new age.

This note of joy and triumph is unmistakable throughout

chapters 40-55, but from chapter 56 onwards the situation seems to be different again. The nation is once more in trouble, and the prophet rebukes its leaders for their shortcomings. At the same time he presents a vision of better times for Jerusalem, and in that respect the spirit of Isaiah is still present. And so it seems that the Book of Isaiah is the work of at least three different people in three different periods of history.

In fact, when we talk of "authorship" in connection with the prophets, it is doubtful whether any of them wrote the books that are named after them. The prophets, like Jesus, sometimes had disciples, and it was the disciples who remembered the prophet's words, repeated them, and applied them to new situations after the prophet's death. There is a story in the Book of Jeremiah (Jer 36) about his scribe Baruch writing down the things that Jeremiah had preached over the years and reading them aloud in a public place as a reminder and warning to the people. The king had them read to him, and contemptuously cut up the scroll and threw it in the fire, whereupon Baruch wrote it all out again. In many cases, however, the writing down of prophecies was probably less formal than this, and a longer period of word of mouth repetition would have intervened. It is to a large extent thanks to this process that we have a Bible at all. Words were only written, circulated and adapted because people saw their relevance in a later situation, a relevance that could usually only be made real by making some adaptation to the original words. By "reading between the lines" and comparing one passage with another we can often have a fascinating insight into this process at work.

When it comes to the New Testament we have already seen that there are problems in the traditional assumption that all the Gospels were written by the people whose names they bear. There is the question as to whether Matthew's Gospel, which seems heavily dependent on Mark, could have been written by one of the Twelve. There is an even bigger question mark over

John's Gospel. This is so different from the others and so theological and mystical in its approach that it is hard to believe it was written by John the fisherman. Moreover, its tone of contemplative devotion, calm faith and gentle love seems out of keeping with the fiery character of John and his brother James, whom Jesus nicknamed "sons of thunder" (Mark 3:17). John was in any case a fairly common name among Jews of that time. There are five books in the New Testament attributed to "John": the Gospel, the three epistles, and the Book of Revelation. We do not know whether they are the work of one person, five different people, or somewhere between.

The doubts expressed by scholars about some of the letters attributed to Paul (Ephesians, Colossians, 2 Thessalonians, 1 and 2 Timothy and Titus) and the Letters of Peter are mostly based on issues of the Greek style and on external evidence that suggests a late date. However, even here the reader who does not know Greek can still see some of the hints. In the Letter to the Ephesians, for example, there is an expression of praise to God that includes the words "to him be glory in the church and in Christ Jesus to all generations, for ever and ever" (Eph 3:21). Can this be the same Paul who advised people not to get married or make any major change in their life because the present world was about to end, or who assumed that he and many of his readers would still be alive to see the return of Christ in glory? (See 1 Cor 7:25-31; 1 Thess 4:15-17).

Again, there is disagreement. Some scholars argue that some of these letters express a theology different from that of Paul, while others believe it was quite possible for Paul himself to change his thinking or to express things in different ways at different times. It is claimed that the Letters to Timothy and Titus reflect the kind of organized hierarchical church that could not have existed in Paul's time, but again we cannot be certain how long it would take for the church to reach that stage of development. It is all a matter of judgment rather than exact science.

For the ordinary reader it is sufficient, and important, to be aware while reading the Bible that things are not always what they seem.

Getting Started

The advantage the biblical scholars have over ordinary readers is not only their extensive knowledge of the background history and culture, the findings of archaeology and so on. It is also that their years of close attention to the text of the Bible have given them a deep familiarity with it. They notice the places where one writer alludes to another, and they get a feeling of the period in history to which a piece of writing belongs. For the ordinary reader this is very difficult, but there are some helps available. A concordance is a very valuable tool. It lists all the words used in the Bible and the places where each word appears. It is very useful for those times when you remember a text but cannot remember where it is in the Bible, but its usefulness goes further than that. It can help us to see what a Bible writer may be alluding to, or to trace a word through the whole Bible and see how its use develops. A Bible dictionary can also be used in this way, and is helpful in understanding the meaning of expressions that at first seem obscure.

How much we invest in commentaries, books of Bible history and so on depends on the time and money we are able or willing to spend. Before buying books of this kind it is always best to consult someone more knowledgeable than yourself, because these books vary considerably in their usefulness. Some commentaries are unreliable. Others give vast amounts of information of little interest to most readers of the Bible but fail to tell you what you really want to know!

Bible study is a fascinating and inexhaustible pursuit, but there are just a few basic facts one needs to know in order to enter into the world of the biblical writers and appreciate something of what they were concerned about. One of these basics is to have a general

picture of the historical framework. The story in the Hebrew scriptures falls roughly into ten episodes:

1. The primeval stories about the creation, Adam and Eve,
    Cain and Abel, the flood and the tower of Babel (Genesis
    1-11).
2. The story of the patriarchs, the first ancestors of the
    Jewish people: Abraham, Isaac, Jacob and his sons
    (Genesis 12-50).
3. The escape of the Israelite slaves from Egypt and their
    journey through the desert to Canaan (Exodus – Joshua).
4. The period during which Israel was a confederation of
    tribes struggling with the other inhabitants of the land
    (Judges, Ruth, 1 Samuel 1-12).
5. The kingdom under Saul and his successors David and
    Solomon (1 Samuel 13:1 – 1 Kings 12:15).
6. The divided kingdoms, Israel in the north and Judah in
    the south (1 Kings 12:16 – 2 Kings 18:12).
7. Judah after the fall of Israel to the Assyrians, until the
    destruction of Jerusalem by the Babylonians (the rest of 2
    Kings).
8. The Exile in Babylon. There is no full account of this, but
    it is reflected in Ezekiel, parts of Jeremiah, Lamentations
    and the stories in the Book of Daniel.
9. The return of some of the Jews from exile, the re-building
    of Jerusalem, and the establishment of the Jewish
    community under the Torah: events that took place after
    Babylon had been taken over by the Persians. Again there
    is no full account of this, and the history is somewhat
    confused. It is told partly in Ezra and Nehemiah, and
    reflected in Isaiah 40-66, Haggai and Zechariah.
10. The continued exile and dispersion of many of the Jews.
    This is reflected in Esther and referred to in some of the
    psalms and some passages in the books of the prophets.

There follows a period often called "between the Testaments", and a little knowledge of this is needed in order to understand the background to the New Testament. Hebrew died out as a spoken language some time after the Exile, giving way to the related language of Aramaic that was spoken in a wider region. Some parts of the books of Ezra and Daniel, and snippets elsewhere in the Hebrew scriptures, are actually written in Aramaic. The Persian Empire was eventually overthrown by Alexander the Great, who by the time he died in 323 BCE ruled over a large area of the Middle East, including Judah. The empire he built did not outlive him, being divided up among his generals, but his conquests had the permanent effect of spreading Greek culture throughout the whole region. The Hebrew scriptures were translated into Greek (the Septuagint), and it was in this version that most of the early Christians knew them. The whole of the New Testament was written in Greek.

After the death of Alexander, Judah was ruled for a time by his successors who became kings of Egypt, but later the power was transferred to the kings of Syria. In 167 BCE the Jews rebelled against the brutal Syrian dictator Antiochus IV: the story is told in the First Book of Maccabees. This resulted in a short period of independence with the descendants of the Maccabees reigning as kings. In 63 BCE Judah and the whole region around it came under the control of the Roman Empire, who governed it partly through vassal kings like the Herods and partly through provincial governors like Pontius Pilate.

The New Testament, as it stands, is divided into two periods: the life of Jesus in the four Gospels and the time of the early church in Acts, the Epistles and Revelation.

These are the phases of history that form the background to the Bible. However, the biblical writings do not in fact fall neatly into these different periods. Something written in one period could be adapted to the different circumstances of another. A story could be imaginatively set in a past era. The Book of Daniel, for instance, is set in the time of the Exile in Babylon in the sixth century BCE, but most of it was probably written four hundred years later, when Jews were struggling against the Syrian kings and the pressure of the Hellenistic way of life. Even the story of Joseph, set in the days of the patriarchs, could well have been written in its present form as an encouragement to Jews living in exile many centuries later. Like Daniel and Esther, it presents the model of a "good Jew" who maintains his or her integrity in a hostile environment and for whom adversity is turned into success. Psalms that rejoice in Jerusalem as the Holy City could have been written in the days when it was the capital and worship centre of the kingdom of Judah, but they could also have been expressing a fond memory, or a hope of future restoration. The detailed descriptions of the "Tabernacle", the tent of worship in the wilderness, are most probably descriptions of Solomon's Temple in Jerusalem or even of the Temple rebuilt after the Exile.

This is true of the New Testament too. The stories of Jesus in the Gospels are heavily influenced, and in some cases perhaps created, by the concerns of the church a generation or so later. One of the most important things to bear in mind in reading the New Testament is that the chronology of the story is not the same as the order of the writings. The letters of Paul come after the Gospels, but were actually written several decades before. So, for instance, Paul's account of the Last Supper (1 Cor 11:23-25) and of the Resurrection appearances (1 Cor 15:3-7) are the earliest accounts we have.

With this general historical framework it is possible to read between the lines and make a guess at the period to which a piece of writing belongs. However, we must always bear in mind that things are not necessarily what they seem. The "episodes" listed above should be seen as *phases*, or as *types of experience* the people of the Bible went through. Often the same kind of experience would recur at different times in history. People would turn to the writings of a prophet of former times, or to an ancient story, to help them make sense of the situation of their own time, and someone would re-write it with a different slant. One well-known example is in the Book of Revelation, where "Babylon" obviously refers to Rome (Rev 17-18). Because of this, it is usually impossible to tell with certainty *when* exactly a passage was written. It is much more relevant to recognize the *type of experience* that it reflects.

We can ask questions like: does this passage reflect a time when the Temple in Jerusalem was still standing and a descendant of David still on the throne? Is it set in the northern kingdom or the southern, or in Babylon? Are the people experiencing freedom and prosperity, or are they oppressed? The same type of situation (release from captivity, victory, defeat, oppression, exile, scattering and gathering, and so on) repeats itself at different times, and we only need to recognize the pattern and enter imaginatively into the experience. If a passage reflects the experience of exile, it does not greatly matter who the exiles were or where or when they were exiled. In fact, this is part of the essential nature of the Bible. The biblical writings only survived because things said and done in one situation were remembered by later generations and seen in a new light in another situation. This process still goes on in synagogues and churches today whenever a preacher takes a text from the scriptures and relates it to a current issue or to the immediate needs and questions of people in the congregation.

With all this in mind, it does not really matter where we start in the Bible. We may choose to read it through from beginning to end, a formidable task, or we may start with familiar and favourite passages. Wherever we are in the Bible it is possible to enter imaginatively into the world of the writers, to respond to the situations they were facing and the passions that moved them, and to join in their ongoing quest.

3

Seeking Wisdom

"But where shall wisdom be found?"
(Job 28:12)

Our culture today has an insatiable thirst for knowledge. We are constantly being informed of new discoveries, of the latest medical breakthrough, the quest for life on other planets, experiments to find the basic building blocks of the universe, and so on. We research not only the world around us but, through the sciences of sociology, economics and psychology, we research ourselves. There is no area of life or the universe, not even God that we are not prepared to investigate scientifically.

The people of the Bible had not developed the techniques of experiment and testing that we have today, but they too were keen to accumulate knowledge. In the description of the wisdom of King Solomon we are told among other things that "he would speak of trees, from the cedar that is in the Lebanon to the hyssop that grows in the wall; he would speak of animals, and birds, and reptiles, and fish" (1 Kgs 4:33). Here is evidence that knowledge of the natural world was highly prized by some at least of the people of the Bible.

The Mysteries of the Universe

These people were as awe-struck as we are by the vastness of the universe and the complexity of life. A psalm that rings bells for us today is the one that says, "When I look at your heavens, the work of your fingers, the moon and the stars that you have established; what are human beings that you are mindful of them..." (Ps 8:3-4). The people who composed those words had no conception of distances measured in light years and stars in trillions, but the universe was just as awesome and mysterious to them as it is to us. Even if they thought the stars were only a few miles up, the inescapable fact about them was that they were inaccessible and uncountable. It is significant too that the psalm asks the question "what are human beings?" without answering it except to make an observation about humankind's amazing power: "Yet you have made them a little lower than God... you have put all things under their feet..." Here is no dry dogmatic statement, but simply an expression of human awe and wonder.

The Bible writers had an overwhelming sense of the mystery of creation. We, with our scientific culture, tend to assume that the things we do not know will eventually be found out by further research. For a pre-scientific culture like that of the Bible there was not this confidence. All sorts of everyday things seemed to be pure miracle. How does the sun rise in the morning and travel across the sky till the evening (Ps 19:4-6)? Where do the rain, the hail and the snow come from: are there storehouses somewhere for them (Job 38:22-30)? How is a baby "knit together" in its mother's womb (Ps 139:13)? The writer of Isaiah 40 is overwhelmed by the way all the stars come out every night, each in its place: it is as if God with his infinite memory calls the roll and ensures that not one is missing (Is 40:26).

Looking at the earth and the sky in all their vastness and at life in all its variety and intricacy, the Bible writers had an overwhelming sense of how infinitely wise the Creator must be. It seemed to them that wisdom must be one of the chief characteristics of God, and that we human beings are pathetically ignorant. The Book of Job has God saying, "Were you there when I laid the foundation of the earth?... Have you entered into the springs of the sea, or walked in the recesses of the deep?.. Have you comprehended the expanse of the earth?" (Job 38:4-18)

In the Apocryphal book called the Wisdom of Solomon, written centuries after Solomon's time, we find an extended version of his prayer for wisdom in which he says to God: "With you is wisdom, she who knows your works and was present when you made the world... for the reasoning of mortals is worthless... we can hardly guess at what is on earth, and what is at hand we find with labour; but who has traced out what is in the heavens?" (Wisd 9:9-16)

Wisdom was thought to be an essential part of the creation of the world: "The LORD by wisdom founded the earth; by understanding he established the heavens" (Prov 3:19). This led on to Wisdom being personified as a kind of companion of God in creation. Proverbs represents Wisdom as saying: "The LORD created me at the beginning of his work, the first of his acts of long ago... when he marked out the foundations of the earth, then I was beside him, like a master worker; and I was daily his delight..." (Prov 8:22-31) Elsewhere in the Book of Proverbs, Wisdom is portrayed as a female character, a woman who stands at her door inviting young men to come into her house and taste the treasures she offers, by contrast with the adulteress who stands like a prostitute at her door and tempts them to their ruin (Prov 7-9: see especially 7:6-17; 9:1-6).

In later times these thoughts about wisdom came to be influenced by Greek philosophy, especially the Stoic concept of the *logos*, the universal principle behind the whole order of the world. In the Wisdom of Solomon, wisdom is called "the fashioner of all things" and described as having "a spirit that is intelligent, holy, unique, manifold, subtle, mobile, clear, unpolluted... a breath of the power of God, and a pure emanation of the glory of the Almighty" (Wisd 7:22ff).

The quotation from Job at the head of this chapter comes from a meditation that dwells on the elusiveness of wisdom. It talks of miners burrowing under the earth in search of precious metals. They explore things that people on the land cannot see, things of which birds and animals can have no conception, but even they cannot find the secret of wisdom. That secret is "hidden from the eyes of all living", and only God "looks to the ends of the earth, and sees everything under the heavens" (Job 28:21, 24). The meditation ends with God saying to humanity: "Truly, the fear of the Lord, that is wisdom; and to depart from evil is understanding" (Job 28:28). This sentiment is found in other places too (Ps 11:10; Prov 9:10; Job 28:28; etc.). It is not a pious cliché, but a thoughtful expression of faith: if God is the Creator of all things, then the key to understanding all things is more likely to be in a respectful recognition of the Creator than in a scornful attitude that boasts of our own intellect and power.

For us today, the issue is not so simple. Many scholars, scientists and people highly respected for their wisdom and humanity are agnostics or atheists. The French scientist Laplace, when he was asked why he had not mentioned God in his work on astronomy, replied "I had no need of that hypothesis". This has become a universal principle for scientists, including those who believe in God. The attempt of some Christian believers to have "intelligent design" taught in schools as a theory to explain the universe is strongly resisted both by scientists and by many religious believers, on the ground that to believe in a Creator God is a matter of faith, not of science. We do not use God as a hypothesis to explain things in nature that seem to have no other explanation. Such a practice leads to the "God of the gaps" whose place gets smaller and smaller as the gaps in our knowledge are filled.

Atheism today is not necessarily an expression of scorn such as we find when the psalmist says "the fool hath said in his heart, there is no God" (Ps 14:1). Many who would call themselves unbelievers are often humbly respectful of the wonder and beauty of the universe and stand in awe of the way in which it has evolved over billions of years. They are often also deeply respectful of their fellow human beings, and it is sometimes this very respect that motivates them to reject religion because it seems so often to abuse and oppress human beings.

There is in fact a basic attitude of respect at the heart of all scientific work. We sometimes talk loosely of the power human beings have over nature, but in fact it is not actually power *over* nature at all: it is power that comes from *understanding* nature and finding new ways to work *with* it. The science and technology that enabled men to land on the moon and enables us now to be in touch with the whole world through our mobile phones, and do all sorts of things our ancestors hardly dreamed of, are based on absolute respect for the way things are. There is no room in them for magic wands, wishful thinking, sloppy planning or the "hope for the best" approach. Everything science and technology achieves is achieved by careful calculation and rigorous testing. The laws of nature are solid realities we cannot change. Only by understanding them and working meticulously in accordance with them do we have the power to control and improve our environment. We could even say that fear comes into it: the expert electrician, unlike the bungling amateur, approaches every task with a healthy fear of the power of electricity and the damage it can do. The designers of spaceships are acutely aware that the physical conditions in outer space are utterly hostile to human life, and that the slightest miscalculation can mean instant death.

This respect for the realities of nature is gaining a new dimension today as we have to come to terms with what human activity is doing to the whole planetary environment. The realistic respect for nature that is vital in the achieving of short-term scientific projects now has to be recognized in the longer term by both scientists and politicians. Many of us may not want to call it "the fear of the Lord", but there is certainly no real wisdom without profound respect for reality and a healthy fear of the implacable forces of the universe.

Crystallized Common Sense

"Wisdom" in the Bible tends to cover a lot of what we today would call "knowledge" or "science", but it also covers what we call "wisdom" in the practical sense, the know-how by which we get along in life and relate to other people. In modern Western culture we are perhaps not so appreciative of the place of elders and wise teachers as our grandparents were. There was a time when, if you wanted advice about cooking or gardening or household repairs you would have a chat with some wise older neighbour. Today you are more likely to buy a little book, pick up a leaflet at the DIY store, or look up a website. This often applies to the problems of life itself. There is a vast literature of "self-help" manuals, and the "agony columns" of newspapers and magazines are a channel through which the "know-how" of life is made accessible to many people.

The ancient Hebrews, like people of all cultures, valued proverbs and wise sayings. There is of course a whole book of the Bible called "Proverbs". Its full title is "The proverbs of Solomon son of David, king of Israel". As we have seen, because of Solomon's reputation for wisdom, all wise sayings tended to be attributed to him. While some sayings were probably produced much later than Solomon's time, others could be even older than Solomon, being part of traditional wisdom coined in ancient times or borrowed from other cultures.

The book begins with a father lecturing his son, exhorting him to take note of what both his father and his mother have taught him, to be honest and not to get mixed up with criminals, to work and not be lazy, and to acknowledge God in everything. Then at the beginning of Chapter 10 there is a new heading, "The proverbs of Solomon", and what follows is largely a random collection. It looks as if someone has kept a scrapbook and just noted proverbs as they heard them. Many of them are very similar to each other.

The book called Ecclesiasticus, or the Wisdom of Jesus Son of Sirach, in the Apocrypha, is similar to Proverbs, but somewhat more discursive. It expands on common themes of wisdom and morality, such as honouring one's parents, friendship, almsgiving and child rearing, often in a pithy and realistic manner. There is sensible advice about how to behave when invited to a rich man's table: the reader is exhorted not to remark on the abundance of food or to reach for it greedily, to "eat like a human being", and to "be the first to stop eating, for the sake of good manners" (Sir 31:12-18). Much of the book reads like a manual of advice to a young person. There is also a passage about what to do in sickness, advocating a balance between prayer and medicine: "My son, when you are sick do not be negligent, but pray to the Lord, and he will heal you. Give up your faults and direct your hands aright, and cleanse your heart from all sin... and give the physician his place, for the Lord created him" (Sir 38:1-15).

The morality behind both Proverbs and Sirach is straight-forward: they advocate piety, honesty, thrift, and generosity to the poor, and promise that such behaviour will be rewarded. This comes out in proverbs like: "The LORD does not let the righteous go hungry, but he thwarts the craving of the wicked" (Prov 10:3) and "Whoever is kind to the poor lends to the LORD, and will be repaid in full" (Prov 19:17). This theme is taken up in some of the psalms that share this "wisdom" characteristic. For example, the first Psalm ("Blessed is the man that walketh not in the counsel of the ungodly"), and Psalm 37 ("Fret not thyself because of evildoers").

This morality is not strenuous or idealistic. Agur, in Proverbs, prays to God: "give me neither poverty nor riches; feed me with the food that I need, or I shall be full, and deny you... or I shall be poor, and steal..." (Prov 30:8-9). Sirach exhorts his son: "treat yourself well, according to your means... do not deprive yourself of a day's enjoyment... give, and take, and indulge yourself, because in Hades one cannot look for luxury" (Sir 14:11-19). Ecclesiastes juxtaposes two pieces of advice: "Do not be too righteous" and "Do not be too wicked" (Eccles 7:16-17). All this is a very far cry from the righteous passion of the prophets, or the radical challenge of Jesus to a life of courageous love, but it drives home to us the point that the writers of the Bible were not heralds of unquestionable divine truth, but human beings like ourselves, drawing on their experience and the wisdom of others as they tried to understand their life and live it wisely.

The New Testament Paradox of Wisdom

The New Testament introduces a new issue. In the Hebrew and Apocryphal scriptures it is evident that the people who were engaged in the quest for wisdom were mostly people in a comfortable situation. The Book of Ecclesiastes presents the picture of a wealthy king sitting in his palace, unsatisfied and thinking about the meaning of everything (Eccles 2). Sirach quite frankly says: "The wisdom of the scribe depends on the opportunity of leisure; only the one who has little business can become wise. How can one become wise who handles the plough, and who glories in the shaft of a goad, who drives oxen and is occupied with their work, and whose talk is about bulls?" (Sir 38:24-25).

However, the Christian faith was not born in that kind of environment. Jesus was a carpenter, and his first disciples were fishermen. They came from Galilee, which even in the Jewish community was seen as somewhat provincial and uncultured. One of the challenges faced by the early Christians was that in the eyes of sophisticated people in the Hellenistic culture of that time the message about a simple Galilean preacher who had been crucified and had risen from the dead was intellectually a non-starter. We see a glimpse of this in the story of Paul in Athens, and the way in which the philosophical discussion group on the Areopagus invited him to speak to them, listened in a rather patronising way, and ended up sneering (Acts 17:16-34). In his first Letter to the Corinthians, Paul says that when he came to Corinth he did not preach with "lofty words of wisdom", but resolved "to know nothing among you except Jesus Christ, and him crucified" (1 Cor 2:1-2). According to Acts, Corinth was the next place he visited after Athens: perhaps it was his experience there that persuaded him to change his approach.

In this Letter to the Corinthians Paul makes a great point of the paradox of divine and human wisdom. He points out how the message of Christ crucified is foolishness in the eyes of the world: "for since, in the wisdom of God, the world did not know God through wisdom, God decided, through the foolishness of our proclamation, to save those who believe". He goes on to call Jesus "the power of God and the wisdom of God" and to make the paradoxical observation that "God's foolishness is wiser than human wisdom, and God's weakness is stronger than human strength" (1 Cor 1:18-25).

And so for Paul the human quest for wisdom has culminated in this paradox, a paradox not just worked out in theory by a king or a scholar who had the luxury of leisure and books, but the fruit of dramatic and painful experience centred on the figure of Jesus.

At the same time, Paul recognizes the value of deeper spiritual understanding. Having asserted that he determined to know nothing among the Corinthians except "Jesus Christ, and him crucified", he then goes on to say that for mature believers there is nevertheless a higher wisdom, a secret and hidden wisdom of God that we may receive through the guidance of the Holy Spirit. There are things, he says, that "no eye has seen, no ear heard, nor the human heart conceived". It is not easy to see what kind of things he is referring to. The only hints he gives are that they are things "God has prepared for those who love him", that they are "gifts bestowed on us by God", and things that can only be "discerned spiritually" (1 Cor 2:6-16). The fact that the Corinthian church is divided into competing parties is a sure indication that they are not yet ready for this wisdom.

There is a thin dividing line between this kind of thinking and the Gnosticism that was the subject of so much conflict in the early days of Christianity. Gnosticism, as its name implies, focused on knowing. This knowing was seen as esoteric knowledge, learned by being initiated into a kind of secret society. The Gospel of Thomas, which has a strong Gnostic tendency, is introduced with the words: "These are the secret sayings which the living Jesus spoke and which Didymus Judas Thomas wrote down. And he said, 'Whoever finds the interpretation of these sayings will not experience death'". There are many sayings in the Gospel of Thomas that are very close to the teachings of Jesus as presented in the New Testament Gospels, but mostly couched in a more cryptic form. The implication seems to be that these sayings have been preserved within a closed community, and that only a person gifted in a certain way can understand their true meaning.

In the early days of Christianity, there were many similar writings and sects to which the general label of "Gnostic" was attached. It is probably some of these that are attacked in the later New Testament writings. The second Letter to Timothy talks of people not putting up with "sound doctrine" but having "itching ears", choosing teachers to suit their own tastes, and wandering away to myths (2 Tim 4:3-4). The first Letter criticizes those who "occupy themselves with myths and endless genealogies that promote speculation rather than the divine training that is known by faith". Sound Christian instruction, it says, aims for "love that comes from a pure heart, a good conscience, and sincere faith" (1 Tim 1:3-5).

There are elements in "new age" thinking today that are similar to this ancient Gnosticism. Some people describe their beliefs as "esoteric". As in ancient times, so today, there is a huge variety of sects and beliefs that come under this category, but the chief characteristic of most of them is the following of a set of teachings believed to have been handed down secretly from ancient times and revealed only to those who are initiated.

Documents discovered during the twentieth century have taught us more about the ancient Gnostic groups and their beliefs than was previously known. Before these discoveries, almost all we knew about them was through the orthodox Christians writings in opposition to them. Today there has been somewhat of a swing of the pendulum, and some theologians are pointing out elements in Gnosticism that were unjustifiably suppressed or unfairly condemned by the leaders of the early church. Feminist scholars in particular point out the way in which some Gnostic views about the status of women and the feminine aspects of the divine were suppressed as the early church became more completely male-dominated.

However, as far as the biblical quest for wisdom is concerned, the main distinction that needs to be drawn is between two basic types of spirituality. Gnosticism in its many forms focuses on knowledge as the spiritual priority. It says that the way to eternal life, relationship with God (or however the ultimate spiritual goal is termed) is through knowing certain revealed facts or understanding certain truths and principles. What hinders us in attaining the spiritual goal is ignorance, or else the forgetfulness that prevents us from living in the constant awareness of what we know. Gnosticism is often focussed on the contrast between reality as we commonly perceive it and reality as it really is.

The focus of mainstream biblical spirituality, however, is not on knowledge but on faith. Faith, of course, can be interpreted as a kind of knowledge, a matter of believing in certain "revealed" facts. This is the way it is often interpreted by dogmatic believers and the kind of church hierarchies that specialize in condemning "heretics". However, the predominant vein of spirituality in the Bible is one based on faith in the sense of trust in a personal God, a trust that shows itself in practical ways, sometimes in the kind of hopefulness and boldness that reaches for what seems impossible. The chief polarity that concerns this kind of faith is not that of the material world as we perceive it and the spiritual world as it really is, but of the world as it is and the world as God wants it to be. In this kind of spirituality, ethical behaviour is a fundamental element, and wisdom consists in knowing God's will for human life and doing it.

For Jews this means obeying the commandments as given in the Torah. There is a passage in Deuteronomy that contrasts the simplicity and accessibility of God's laws with any notion of esoteric or exotic knowledge:

"Surely, this commandment that I am commanding you today is not too hard for you, nor is it too far away. It is not in heaven, that you should say, 'Who will go up to heaven for us, and get it for us so that we may hear it and observe it?' Neither is it beyond the sea, that you should say, 'Who will cross to the other side of the sea for us, and get it for us so that we may hear it and observe it?' No, the word is very near to you; it is in your mouth and in your heart for you to observe" (Deut 30:11-14).

The meaning of this reference to the mouth and the heart is probably much more down-to-earth than we might think. In a largely illiterate society, the only way most people could learn the laws was by constantly repeating them aloud until they knew them by heart. Elsewhere in the same book the people are told to teach the commandments to their children and to talk about them constantly as they go about their daily life (Deut 6:7). The general tendency of Jewish and Christian thinking is to see knowing the ways of God as something open to everybody rather than guarded by any kind of elite.

The Epistle of James echoes much of the wisdom literature of the Jewish scriptures. It exhorts anyone lacking wisdom to pray for it wholeheartedly in faith (Jas 1:5-7). At the same time it draws the contrast between the self-glorifying "wisdom" of the world and the true wisdom that is peaceable, gentle and full of mercy (Jas 3:13-18). While echoing the principle that "the fear of the LORD is the beginning of wisdom", it is also suggesting the wisdom of love as opposed to "worldly wisdom".

For Paul, true wisdom seems to be something different from intellectual understanding. It is bound up with his sense of a personal relationship with God through a real, practical identification with Christ in his suffering and death. When he talks of his own spiritual aspirations, the way he expresses it is in words like "I want to know Christ and the power of his resurrection and the sharing of his sufferings" (Phil 3:10). This is not knowledge of facts or truths, but knowledge in the sense of experience, a knowledge he hopes to gain not so much by studying as by living as a disciple of Christ.

And so, notwithstanding all the emphasis on wisdom that it shares with other traditions, we can say that Jewish and Christian spirituality is fundamentally not a matter of "*what* you know" but of "*Who* you know", not intellectual knowledge, but knowing God as we know a person.

4

The Mystery of God

"If . . . they ask me, 'What is his name?' what shall I say to them?"
(Ex 3:13)

"Theology means rational wrestling with the mystery. But all rational wrestling with this mystery, the more serious it is, can lead only to its fresh and authentic interpretation and manifestation as a mystery. For this reason it is worth our while to engage in this rational wrestling with it. If we are not prepared for this we shall not even know what we are saying when we say that what is at issue here is God's mystery."
(Karl Barth, *Church Dogmatics* I,1, p.368)

The question of God is more alive than ever today. Can we believe in God? Is belief in God compatible with a rational scientific view of the universe? How do we maintain faith in a loving and righteous God in the face of all the bad things that happen in the world? And perhaps the most fundamental question: what do we mean by "God" anyway?

Many believers talk confidently of the "evidence" for God's existence. They point to the beauty and complexity of the universe and draw the simple conclusion that there must be a Creator. They tell stories of miracles that seem impossible to deny. They testify to their own experience of answered prayer.

Even among religious thinkers today there is some embarrassment about this. They do not feel happy with a God who interferes in the course of nature. They argue that in any case a God who could be proved would not be God. If there is a God, that God must be present everywhere and in everything: we should not look for "evidence" in particular things. Faith by definition is not certainty. It is a perspective by which we see the world, an attitude in which we live our lives. For Christians especially, there is the argument that God is above all a loving God, and the essence of love is that it is vulnerable. It cannot force a response, but can only wait for it. If God could prove his existence beyond any doubt, we would be compelled to acknowledge and obey him, but this would not be love.

On the other hand, there are determined atheists today who not only dismiss simple, traditional faith as superstition, but are just as contemptuous of faith in these more subtle and nuanced expressions. Their question is: if God does not visibly, tangibly *do* things that make a difference in this world, what sense does it make to talk of God at all? What is the point of believing in a God whose very nature is to be hidden, a God whose presence is never clearly shown, and who cannot be seen to be actually doing anything? What difference would it make to abandon these attempts to justify and explain away the lack of evidence and simply state the obvious (to them) fact that there is no god?

In spite of the powerful logic of these arguments, the experience of millions of committed religious believers, and of many other thinking and sensitive people, is that somehow God won't go away. People have an inescapable feeling that there is a spiritual reality in the universe. Science deals with the "how" questions, but many of us want to ask the "why" questions. We feel there must be a meaning, a point, to our own life and to the existence of the world. We cannot help believing that we are more than the sum of our parts. Physics and chemistry can explain so much, even emotions and the workings of the brain, but we each still experience ourselves as a living person with character, relationships, ideas and dreams. Where does all this come from, and what does it mean?

Of course very few people today imagine the world being controlled by an old man with a beard sitting on a throne in the sky, but many of us have the sense of an infinitely mysterious, indefinable ultimate reality whom we label "God", and we believe it is worthwhile to explore this reality, to try to understand and know this God better. We want to pray, or at least to meditate, and to walk the risky path of faith.

Many believers insist that the Bible contains the answers to all these questions. Others have turned to the Bible looking for the answers and been puzzled and disappointed. The Bible seems to speak a language that is alien to their spiritual search, and so they turn away from it and look elsewhere. Much of this disillusionment with the Bible, or complete dismissal of it, comes from the assumption that the Bible is *supposed* to have all the answers. In reality, however, the Bible is not a manual of information about God. It is the long, rambling but very lively record of an ongoing quest for God. Its writings come out of the attempts of people within the Judaeo-Christian stream of culture to make sense of their experience and to maintain their faith. The people who wrote it were, like all of us, searching for truth, trying to work out the meaning of their life experience, and reaching out for the God they wanted to believe in but often found hard to understand. Once we break free from the habit of thinking of the Bible as a book of answers, and start noticing the questions, we can begin to realise that we and they are fellow travellers in the ongoing quest for God. It is not a monologue spoken by God, but a human conversation that still goes on.

Though the Bible is often called "the word of God", very little of it is actually in the form of words spoken by God. In fact, already in the third chapter of Genesis we find words spoken by the serpent to induce Eve to distrust God. In the Book of Job, and in the story of the temptations of Jesus, we find words uttered by Satan! Most of the Bible consists not of words spoken *by* God but of the words of human beings talking *about* God, or talking *to* God. Nor is talking to God always prayer and praise: it is often words of anger, the words of people questioning God and arguing with him. The Bible is not so much a text book about

God as a kind of ongoing journal of the quest for God.

A Fearful Mystery

Most of the Bible stories we heard as children portrayed God as a rather human-like but all-powerful person who appears from time to time and talks with people. This image of God is certainly present in the Bible. We have already seen it in the story of Adam and Eve. Later we find God giving detailed instructions to Noah about the building of the ark, and personally shutting the door when Noah, his family and the animals are safely inside (Gen 7:16). Abraham, Moses, Jonah and other characters have conversations with God. In passages like this, and indeed in some sense throughout the Bible, God is not an abstract idea but a person with whom human beings can converse as with another human being.

However, there are other stories in which God is a frightening, unpredictable power. Just after the inspiring story of how God appeared to Moses in a burning bush and commissioned him to go to Pharaoh and demand the release of the Hebrew slaves, there is a very odd little story (Ex 4:24-26) that tells how God met him on the way back to Egypt and tried to kill him. The situation was only saved by Moses' wife cutting off her son's foreskin and touching Moses' feet with it: or perhaps not his feet, because "feet" could be a euphemism for the genitals. The meaning of this story is very obscure, but it shows how for the ancient Hebrews the benevolence of God could not be taken for granted. God could be experienced as a destructive and hostile force.

There is another story of how, when David was having the Ark of God transported to Jerusalem, one of the men accompanying it saw it being shaken on its ox-cart and put out his hand to steady it. Well-meaning as the action was, "the anger of the LORD was kindled" against him for daring to touch the Ark, and he was struck dead on the spot (2 Sam 6:6-7). This induced David to abandon the project for the time being and leave the Ark at a place nearby: it was too dangerous to handle. It was only three months later, when he found that the family with whom the Ark had been left was prospering and obviously blessed by God, that David thought it safe to resume the process of bringing it to Jerusalem.

It is stories like these that remind us that the ancient Israelites, with all their belief in a righteous, consistent God and their confidence that God had chosen them as his people and entered into a covenant with them, never quite lost the sense of fear and uncertainty about this mysterious character called "God". God, like our experience of life itself, can never be finally understood.

It is clear that the God of the Bible writers was not always a simple concept. There emerges here and there a profound sense of the mystery of God's being. This happens not so much in philosophical theology as in the subtlety of story-telling. One very interesting and teasing example is the story of how Abraham and his wife Sarah were told they would have a child (Gen 18). In this story "the LORD" seems to appear to Abraham in the form of three men, but he seems uncertain as to whether to address him/them in the singular or the plural. We quote from the King James Bible so as to make clear the alternation between the singular "thou" and "thee" and the plural "ye" and "you":

> "My lord, if now I have found favour in thy sight, pass not away, I pray thee, from thy servant: let a little water, I pray you, be fetched, and wash your feet, and rest yourselves under the tree: and I will fetch a morsel of bread, and comfort ye your hearts: for therefore are ye come to your servant. And they said, So do, as thou hast said."

After they have eaten, "they" ask where Sarah is, but when Abraham answers, "he" gives the promise that Sarah will have a son. Sarah then laughs, and "the LORD" asks why she is laughing. After this, "the men" turn away towards Sodom, while

Abraham remains "standing before the LORD". Was it the LORD who appeared to Abraham, or three men, or one man, or three men and the LORD? It is of course possible that this confusion results from the weaving together of different versions of the story. On the other hand, it could be that the final editor deliberately kept the inconsistencies in order to convey this sense of the mystery of God.

This mystery is also profoundly expressed in the story of the encounter of Moses with God at the burning bush. When Moses asks what God's name is, he receives the answer, "I AM WHO I AM" (Ex 3:14). The phrase is partly a play on the divine name Yahweh and its similarity with the Hebrew verb "to be". Because of the way the tenses work in the Hebrew language, this "I am who I am" could also be translated "I will be who I will be". The name could mean that God is incomparable, and no definition can ever be adequate. It could be that he simply refuses to give his name. In that culture, knowing the name of a god gave a person some power over the god, and God is perhaps here denying any such power to human beings. It could also mean that we will never stop being surprised by who God is, that God will be who God will be. Or it could mean that God has the freedom to be what God wants to be. This apparently simple statement is therefore deeply ambiguous and open to creative interpretation.

A further very profound experience is described in a less well-known story (Ex 33:18-23), when Moses asks to see the full glory of God. The response he receives is: "I will make all my goodness pass before you, and will proclaim before you the name, YHWH". This in itself is very suggestive. There is a sense in which all we human beings really have of God is the *name* – the simple fact that we talk about God and interpret our life and the world by using some such word as "God" or "the Lord". Only a tiny minority of religious believers claim to have literally had a tangible meeting with God such as seeing a vision or hearing a voice. For the great majority, faith is a matter of habitually inter-preting the whole of life through the mental concept of "God", which in a sense is just a word. Perhaps this passage is implying that human beings cannot see God's glory, they can only hear God's name. This seems to be borne out in the next chapter, in which as God passes before Moses, he proclaims: "The LORD, the LORD, a God merciful and gracious, slow to anger, and abounding in steadfast love and faithfulness... yet by no means clearing the guilty..." (Ex 34:6-7). To hear God's name and know something of God's nature is the most we can expect.

There are other places in the Bible where the "name" of God seems to stand for God himself, or perhaps for the only way we human beings can meet directly with God. The Temple in Jerusalem is sometimes described as the dwelling place of God. It is said of Jerusalem: "God is in the midst of her; she shall not be moved" (Ps 46:5). Solomon, at the dedication of the Temple, says to God: "I have built you an exalted house, a place for you to dwell in forever" (1 Kgs 8:13). Further on in the same chapter, however, doubts are expressed: "But will God indeed dwell on the earth? Even heaven and the highest heaven cannot contain you, much less this house that I have built" (1 Kgs 8:27). The Temple is then re-defined as the place of which God has said "My name shall be there" (1 Kgs 8:29), and this is the way it is referred to in the rest of that long prayer.

In the story about Moses, however, there is a passage (Ex 33:19-23) where God does grant him a visual experience. Here, as in many other places, different versions of the story are woven together. God says to Moses, "you cannot see my face; for no one shall see me and live". He says that he will put Moses in a cleft in the rock, and cover it with his hand as he passes by. Then he will take away his hand, and Moses will see his back. This picture that on one level looks rather quaint, even comic, is in fact very profound. It seems to suggest that we never see God directly: what we see is just some aspect of God, or perhaps just a sign that God *has been* with us. This experience is echoed in the New Testament story of the two disciples who meet the risen Jesus on the road to Emmaus. As soon as they realise it is Jesus, he is no longer with them, but they look back on the experience and say, "Were not our hearts burning within us while he was talking to us on the road?" (Luke 24:32) A similar experience is expressed in the very popular modern meditation *Footprints*, where the believer looks back and is told that the places where there is only one set of footprints are the times of particular trouble, when they were being carried by God. The sense of the presence of God is rarely direct: it is more likely to be indirect, partial and retrospective.

Singular or Plural?

There is an ambiguous singular/plural element in God as sometimes portrayed in the Hebrew scriptures. We have not only the story of the three mysterious visitors to Abraham, but also the fact that one of the Hebrew words for God, *Elohim*, is plural in form. In the story of creation, *Elohim* says, "Let us make humankind in our image" (Gen 1:26). After Adam and Eve have taken the forbidden fruit, God (here called *YHWH Elohim*) says, "See, the man has become like one of us" (Gen 3:22), and when people start building the tower of Babel, God says, "Let us go down, and confuse their language there" (Gen 11:7). It is not clear to whom these words are addressed. Is there a sort of divine council? Is God talking to angels, or to himself/themselves? Or is it just a figure of speech, a kind of "royal we"?

There are also aspects of God that at times seem to take on a life of their own. We have already seen that the "name" of God sometimes has this kind of function: it becomes in a sense the presence of God himself. The "angel of the LORD", too, has a similar function. The word translated "angel", both in Hebrew and in Greek, means "messenger". It could sometimes mean a human messenger rather than a supernatural being, but this "angel" seems often to be synonymous with God himself. In the story of Abraham being willing to sacrifice his son Isaac, it is "God" who commands him to do it, but it is "the angel of the LORD" who stops him doing it, not by appearing this time but by calling to him from Heaven (Gen 22:1,11). Perhaps even more significantly, the very story in which the name YHWH is revealed to Moses begins by saying that "the angel of the LORD" appeared to him as fire in a bush (Ex 3:2).

The "spirit of God" or "the spirit of the LORD" also features frequently in the Hebrew scriptures. There may be a reference to this spirit at the very beginning, where it is said that "the Spirit of God moved upon the face of the waters" (Gen 1:2, AV). However, the word translated "spirit" can also mean "wind", and "wind of God" could be an idiomatic expression for a very strong wind – in some parts of England people use the phrase "a God-Almighty wind". Again, the ambiguity could well be deliberate. We are on surer ground when we come to the words of Pharaoh, who according to the story is so impressed by the wisdom of Joseph and his ability to interpret dreams that he calls him "one in whom is the spirit of God" (Gen 41:37). This spirit of God is seen in other places too as the giver of skill and wisdom (Ex 31:1 etc.), as giving Samson his strength (Judg 14:6.19; 15:14), and as inspiring the prophets (Num 11:25-29; Is 61:1; Joel 2:28-29).

This last understanding of the "Spirit of God" becomes very prominent in the New Testament. John the Baptist announces that one is coming after him who will baptize people not with water but with "the Holy Spirit and fire" (Matt 3:11 etc.). When Jesus is baptized, the Spirit of God descends on him in the form of a dove (Matt 3:16 etc.). Particularly in Luke's Gospel, Jesus is said to be "full of the Spirit" (Luke 4:1) or "filled with the power of the Spirit" (Luke 4:14). Luke goes on to tell how the Spirit filled the apostles on the day of Pentecost (Acts 2:4) and on later occasions (Acts 4:31; 7:55 etc.). It is evident too, particularly from the letters of Paul, that the early Christians saw all kinds of extra-ordinary abilities as gifts of the Holy Spirit (1 Cor 12 etc.). In the development of Christian doctrine, mostly after New Testament times, the Spirit was joined with the Father and the Son as part of the Holy Trinity.

There is one more figure that is sometimes referred to as a kind of divine being. In the Wisdom literature, as we have seen, "Wisdom" often appears as a distinct being closely associated with God, and usually a female figure. It is interesting that when Jesus echoes the words of Sirach about taking up the yoke of wisdom and finding rest (Sir 51:23-27; Matt 11:28-30) it is in close association with his saying that "no one knows the Son except the Father, and no one knows the Father except the Son" (Matt 11:27). Jesus seems here to be identified with that Wisdom that was with God from the beginning. The Gospel of John identifies Jesus with "the Word" (*logos*), a concept that seems to be associated with Greek philosophy and is very close to that of Wisdom.

The Battle for Monotheism

None of this apparently plural way of talking about God comes anywhere near implying that the early Israelites or the later Jews saw themselves as worshipping more than one God. The "name", the "angel", the "spirit" and "wisdom" are all aspects, or even titles, of the one God. This God, according to the prophets and leaders whose teaching has come down to us, tolerated no rival.

It is not quite clear how far they were monotheists in the sense of believing that only one God exists. In early times they probably assumed that there were other gods. For example, there is the story (1 Sam 5:1-5) of how the Philistines stole the Ark of God in a battle against the Israelites, but when they placed it in their temple the statue of their god Dagon fell on its face. They set it up again, but the next morning they found that it had fallen again and was broken. This seems to imply that Dagon was a real god, but was overcome by the power of Israel's God.

One of the psalms asks, "what god is so great as our God?" (Ps 77:13). He is also called "the God of gods" (Ps 136:2) and "a great King above all gods" (Ps 95:3). Psalm 82 describes God taking his place in the divine council and addressing "the gods", telling them that, gods though they may be, they will be punished for their injustice towards the poor by dying "like mortals". It is possible that "gods" here is a metaphorical term for powerful earthly rulers, or perhaps for semi-divine beings like angels, who can be bad as well as good. At the same time, this psalm ends with the prayer, "Rise up, O God, judge the earth; for all the nations belong to you!" And so it is clear that for those who sang this psalm, whatever other gods the nations may have, there is but one God in charge of the world.

The gods of the surrounding nations – Rimmon of the Aramaeans (2 Kgs 5:18), Astarte of the Sidonians, Chemosh of the Moabites (1 Kgs 11:33) and so on – are often mentioned in the Hebrew scriptures, but the chief rivals to the God revealed to Israel in the desert were the indigenous Canaanite Baals (sometimes referred to as a singular, Baal). These were the gods of the land who were thought to make the soil fertile and produce a rich harvest if the proper sacrifices were made to them.

The God presented in the Hebrew scriptures was particularly associated with the story of the desert wanderings after the escape from Egypt, the God who had revealed himself and given his commandments to Moses on Mount Sinai. Whatever the historical truth about the Exodus (and archaeologists doubt that it happened just as the Bible tells it), it was this story that largely shaped the prophets' imagination of God. It is understandable that this God of the desert, who had fed the people with manna from Heaven, would seem distant and unconnected with the agricultural and urban life of many Israelites. The Book of Deuteronomy makes much of this theme. It is a kind of extended sermon put into the mouth of Moses. He reminds the people of how God has led them through the desert and cared for them, but then he points out that once they have entered the Promised Land their conditions of life will be very different. They will be growing crops and owning vineyards, mining for iron and copper, building houses and accumulating money. He warns them against saying to themselves, "My power and the might of my own hand have gained me this wealth". "Remember the LORD your God", he says to them, "for it is he who gives you power to get wealth" (Deut 8).

There is an interesting parallel here with the situation of religion in Western society today. Our nomadic past is now too distant to remember, but for many of us religion is stuck with our agricultural past. It is inseparably associated with country churches, harvest festivals and the beauty of the trees and flowers. Hardly any of our hymns and liturgies mention mines and factories, much less computers and financial markets: these things seem somehow to have nothing to do with God. Perhaps we need some new Deuteronomy to convince us that God is as real in our post-industrial economy as he ever was to our rural ancestors.

The religious struggle continued throughout the history of the two kingdoms. One of its dramatic climaxes is the story of the contest between Elijah and hundreds of prophets of Baal and Asherah on Mount Carmel (1 Kgs 18:20-40). Elijah challenges the prophets to lay a sacrificial bull on an altar and call upon Baal to send down fire from Heaven to burn it. After they have been calling on Baal all day, to the accompaniment of Elijah's taunts, he rebuilds the altar of the Lord, lays a bull on it, drenches it with water and prays, and sure enough, fire sweeps down from Heaven and burns not only the bull but even the stones of the altar. The religious struggle reflected a political one. The Bible story tells how Solomon and the other kings formed alliances with neighbouring kingdoms that often involved inter-marriage. Princesses of powerful royal households would naturally be able to demand the facilities to worship their own gods and build altars for them in Israel and Judah, as is specifically said of Solomon's wives (1 Kgs 11:1-8). The prophets could well have been political dissidents who wanted Israel to maintain its independence and its distinctive character by sticking strictly to its own God. They were probably a minority in their time, and it may have been only after Israel collapsed and Judah became more powerful that strict monotheism, with Jerusalem as the only permitted place for the offering of sacrifices, gained the upper hand.

Monotheism as such reaches its full-blown acknowledgement in the second part of Isaiah, which belongs to the period of the Exile in Babylon. It is there that we find statements like "Before me no god was formed, nor shall there be any after me", and "I am the LORD, and there is no other; besides me there is no god" (Is 43:10; 45:5; etc.). As for the other "gods", "they are all a delusion; their works are nothing; their images are empty wind" (Is 41:29). The phrase "besides me there is no god" is repeated several times (Is 44:6; 45:5.21 etc.), as if the prophet was rejoicing in the negative, a kind of liberating atheism in relation to all the powers that were looked upon as divine. We could read this today as a challenge not only to the apparently irresistible "realities" of politics and economics, but even to the mental images by which we try to define the God who is beyond all definition.

By the time of Jesus idolatry, in the sense of literally setting up shrines and offering prayer and sacrifice to other gods, was no longer an issue among the Jewish people: to be a Jew meant to stand implacably opposed to the idol worship of the surrounding Greek and Roman culture. The mission of Jesus was to call the Jewish people themselves to a much more radical recognition of the absolute claims of the one God. He encouraged people to trust in God for their security and not in material possessions. It was an either-or: "You cannot serve God and Mammon" (Matt 6:24). In these days when Christians agonize over the challenge of other faiths and argue about how exclusive Christian faith is meant to be, it is worth noting that the only religion Jesus specifically condemned was the worship of money!

Maker of Good and Evil?

One of the uncompromisingly monotheistic statements in Isaiah says: "I am the LORD, and there is no other. I form light and create darkness, I make weal and create woe" (Is 45:6-7).

This points to an issue in which we today can often find be disturbed by the biblical view of God. Most of the writers of the Hebrew scriptures seem to have had no hesitation in regarding God as the source of all things, whether good or bad. In the Book of Ruth Naomi, returning to Bethlehem after losing her husband and her two sons, says: "The LORD has dealt harshly with me, and the Almighty has brought calamity on me" (Ruth 1:21). Hannah's childlessness is explained by saying "the LORD had closed her womb" (1 Sam 1:5-6). Afterwards, when her prayer for a child has been granted, she sings a song of praise in which she says: "The LORD kills and brings to life; he brings down to Sheol[1] and raises up. The LORD makes poor and makes rich, he brings low, he also exalts" (1 Sam 2:6-7).

When King Saul started to fall into fits of melancholy, it is said that "the spirit of the LORD departed from Saul, and an evil spirit from the LORD tormented him". This could be interpreted as the narrator showing how Saul was being punished for his disobedience, but in the next sentence we are told that Saul's servants, who presumably would be more inclined to flatter him than to join in the blame, said to him: "See now, an evil spirit from God is tormenting you" (1 Sam 16:14-15). It seems that anything that had no simple down to earth explanation, whether good or bad, was seen as "from God".

Job, in his suffering, assumes that it is God who is afflicting him: "the arrows of the Almighty are in me... the terrors of God are arrayed against me" (Job 6:4). He asks God why he is tormenting him so much and will not leave him alone (Job 7:11-20). At another point, he says of God:

"It is all one; therefore I say, he destroys both the blameless and the wicked. When disaster brings sudden death, he mocks at the calamity of the innocent. The earth is given into the hand of the wicked; he covers the eyes of its judges – if it is not he, who then is it?" (Job 9:22-24)

This is an unresolved paradox in the biblical picture of God. While asserting on the one hand that God is righteous and good, the writers of the Hebrew scriptures often seem to portray God as morally indifferent, inflicting bad things on people sometimes for no apparent reason. The question still haunts believers in God today: if God does not cause these things to happen, who does?

One answer is to believe that there is another power in the world: Satan, the Devil. The introduction to the Book of Job sets a scene in which Satan casts doubt on the genuineness of Job's piety, and God gives him permission to afflict Job in order to test him. However, in the main body of the book it never seems to occur to Job or any of his friends that his suffering is the work of Satan: it is attributed to God. Moreover, when at the end of the book God commends Job and restores his health and fortune, there is no mention of Satan having to acknowledge that he was wrong. The issue is between God, Job and his friends, and Satan's part in the story seems to have been forgotten. Job's relations visit him with gifts to comfort him "for all the evil that the LORD had brought upon him" (Job 42:11). Even in the beginning of the book, of course, Satan only inflicts misfortune and pain on Job because God has given him permission to do so.

Satan is not actually a major character in the Hebrew scriptures. In the Book of Job he has a polite though adversarial relationship with God. In fact, in the Hebrew he is called "the Satan" (that is the Accuser) and is one of the "sons of God", implying perhaps that he has some kind of official function in the heavenly court, a kind of "counsel for the prosecution". He appears again briefly in the Book of Zechariah (Zech 3:1-2) in the role of an accuser.

The idea of a force directly and totally opposed to God probably came into Jewish thinking after the Exile through the influence of Persian religion, with its stark contrast between light and darkness. It is interesting, for instance, to compare the two versions of the story of David conducting a census of the people, an action seen as a sin. In the older history (2 Sam 24:1) we are told that "the anger of the LORD was kindled against Israel" and he incited David to conduct the census so that Israel would suffer. In the later books of Chronicles, however (1 Chr 21:1) it was Satan who "stood up against Israel, and incited David".

Satan and his army of devils feature largely in the story of Jesus, but it is always quite clear that his power is not nearly equal to that of God. He is doomed to be defeated. The healing activities of Jesus are often described as the casting out of evil spirits, and as a sign that Satan's power has lost its sting (Mark 3:22-27; Luke 10:18 etc.). In John's Gospel the crucifixion itself is seen as the moment when "the ruler of this world will be driven out" (John 12:31). Jesus was tempted by Satan during his forty days in the wilderness, but it is said that he was driven there by the Spirit of God: Satan was simply serving God's purpose (Matt 4:1; Mark 1:12-13; Luke 4:1-2).

If we talk of God as "almighty", the concept of Satan does not in the end solve the problem of evil. Neither Judaism nor Christianity preaches a dualistic view of the world in which the force of good and the force of evil are equivalent. For both faiths it is quite clearly God who is in charge, and if there is a Devil he exists and acts only because God allows him to. But then why does God allow it?

We find it distasteful today to talk of God inflicting pain and misfortune, but there is still a dilemma we cannot escape. If God is the Creator and Ruler of the whole world, do we have any better explanation of things than the assumption of the Hebrew scriptures that one God is in some sense responsible for everything that happens? If we are happy to talk about creation showing the beauty, the goodness and the generosity of God, we still somehow have to take into account the frightening, impersonal, apparently uncaring aspect of the universe. Believers do not have a charmed life: as the writer of Ecclesiastes says, the wisest and most civilized of human beings shares with the wild animals the stark fact of mortality (Eccles 3:19-21). The natural world is not designed for the protection of human beings: there are all kinds of dangerous animals, reptiles and insects that kill people or cause them extreme suffering, not to mention the viruses against which we wage a constant battle. It is conceivable that a virus could one day evolve which would spread so easily and rapidly that the whole human race would be destroyed. We also know more today about how vulnerable the planet itself is. Earthquakes happen because the planet's surface is still in an unsettled state. The earth itself is only one of innumerable bodies moving in space, and there is always the possibility that a collision could annihilate the very planet we live on. There is that about nature that seems entirely indifferent to the welfare of human beings or to any moral standards.

Bad things happen, and if we believe in God at all we are bound to be tempted to echo Job's question (Job 9:24): if it is not God who makes these things happen, who then is it? This question seems to be answered in the Book of Job by the speech of God in the closing chapters, the message of which is that God has made the world and everything in it, that we human beings are a very small part of that creation, and that God does not need to explain himself to us. And yet, as the last chapter shows, that same God listens to us, respects our questions, and engages in conversation with us. We, like the writers of the Bible, are still wrestling with the ultimate mystery of God's being.

Three in One?

For Christians there is a unique dimension to the mystery of God: the centring of the experience of God in a human being, Jesus of Nazareth. Here it is more evident than ever that the biblical writers were engaged in a quest, each coming to a different expression of the significance of Jesus. The full-blown doctrine of the Trinity, and the relationship of humanity and divinity in Christ, was to be the subject of fierce debate for centuries to come.

In the first Letter of John there is a rather cryptic statement that the divine credentials of Jesus are borne out by three witnesses: the Spirit, the water and the blood. In the King James Version this is preceded by the statement: "For there are three that bear record in heaven, the Father, the Word, and the Holy Ghost: and these three are one" (1 John 5:7). However, this only appears in a few manuscripts, and even then in different wording. It has been dropped by all the modern translations, though the New Revised Standard and New International versions mention it in a footnote. This is in all probability a sentence added to the original by one or more zealous theologians who were determined that there should be at least one text in the Bible that straightforwardly asserted the doctrine of the Trinity. The reality of the New Testament is rather different. It seems that the writers are struggling with an experience and a conviction that is difficult to put into words.

The relationship of Jesus to God is ambiguous in the Gospels. He himself seems not generally to have welcomed the expression "Son of God" but to have preferred "Son of Man", a title whose meaning is very difficult to pin down. According to Matthew's Gospel, he was overjoyed when Peter called him "the Messiah, the Son of the living God" (Matt 16:16). However, in the versions of this story in Mark and Luke the expression "Son of God" is not used, and the response of Jesus is much less enthusiastic (Mark 8:29-30; Luke 9:20-21). All three of these Gospels mention the question put to Jesus at his trial as to whether he was the Son of God. In Matthew and Luke he says something like "you say so" (Matt 26:63-64; Luke 22:70), but in Mark he says simply "I am" (Mark 14:61-62). This, however, is not quite certain, since the manuscripts vary at this point. In any case, the expression "Son of God" can have a wide range of meanings: it is applied in the Hebrew scriptures to the king of Israel (2 Sam 7:14 etc.) and to Israel as a nation (Hos 11:1), and in the New Testament to Christian believers (John 1:12; 1 John 3:1). In the Beatitudes Jesus says that peacemakers will be called "children of God" (Matt 5:9), and Paul says that those who belong to Christ have been given the "Spirit of adoption" and are children and heirs of God (Rom 8:15-17).

It is in John's Gospel that Jesus is most clearly presented as divine. The opening verses, using the concept of *logos*, which would have particular philosophical associations for people educated in Greek culture, says that the "Word" which was in the beginning with God, and was God, was made flesh and lived among us (John 1:1-3,14). The writer stops short of saying that *God* was made flesh. He goes on to say: "No one has ever seen God. It is God the only Son, who is close to the Father's heart *(literally, in the bosom of the Father)*, who has made him known" (John 1:18). Later Jesus is represented as saying to Nicodemus, "God so loved the world that he gave his only Son" (John 3:16) – a statement that is echoed by Paul (Rom 8:3). The New Testament generally seems more at home talking of God sending his Son into the world than of God actually becoming a human being.

Later in John's Gospel, Jesus says "the Father and I are one" and "the Father is in me and I am in the Father" (John 10:30.37), but this is in a context of talking about the things that Jesus does and teaches. It may simply mean that Jesus is so fully identified with God's character and purpose that he can say "whoever has seen me has seen the Father" (John 14:10). All this is open to different interpretations, but it falls short of the full doctrine of the Trinity as it was developed in the first few centuries of Christian history. The most unequivocal statement of the divinity of Jesus is on the lips of Thomas, who had not believed Jesus was alive until he saw for himself, and then said, "My Lord and my God!" (John 20:28) Some commentators believe that even here Thomas was not directly addressing Jesus as God, but praising God because Jesus was alive. Whatever the words mean, they are not a cold theological statement but a spontaneous expression of strong feeling. In fact, the writer of John's Gospel, like most of the Bible writers, is not basically concerned with doctrine but with experience.

The Letter to the Hebrews has its own particular slant on Jesus and his relation to God. First it says that he is the perfect image of God, "the reflection of God's glory and the exact imprint of God's very being" (Heb 1:3). But then it presents him in a more human way than many other parts of the New Testament. He was made "perfect through sufferings" (Heb 2:10) – suggesting perhaps that he was not already quite perfect. He is able to understand those going through testing or temptation because he was "in every respect... tested as we are, yet without sin" (Heb 4:15). As a man he "offered up prayers and supplications, with loud cries and tears, to the one who was able to save him from death". He "learned obedience through what he suffered" (Heb 5:7-8). Here is a view of Jesus as one who, while perfectly revealing God, is quite definitely a human being.

The whole New Testament view of Jesus is a deep paradox. Its writers in their different ways are trying to convey their belief that God, who in most religious thought is highly exalted, glorious and almighty, is supremely revealed in Jesus, a human being who mingles with the outcasts of society and is identified with them by being condemned to death. The Creator of life is revealed in a dying man, the holy God in a condemned law breaker who dies asking God why he has forsaken him.

The doctrines of the Christian church have tried to tie this all up neatly in statements that can be imposed on people as orthodoxy, but within the New Testament the mystery is still alive and being freely explored. As with most of the Bible, we need not strive to fit everything into a consistent pattern and find out what "the Bible" says. It is much more fruitful to try to enter into what the individual writers are trying to express, and join them in the ongoing exploration of the subtle, elusive nature of God.

A Person or Not?

Many spiritually minded people today are reluctant to talk about "God" as a person. They prefer to talk about "spirit", or "the universe", or some kind of force or essence. The influence of Buddhism is very strong in today's spirituality. We tend to think that if it is legitimate to speak about "God" at all we mean the God who is within us, the God whom the Christian theologian Paul Tillich calls "the Ground of our being".

There is an element of this kind of thinking in the Bible. In John's Gospel, Jesus talks about his disciples being in him as he is in God (John 14:20; 15:4; 17:21-23 etc.). Paul talks of believers being in Christ and of Christ being in them (Rom 8:1.10). Of himself he says, "I have been crucified with Christ; and it is no longer I who live, but it is Christ who lives in me" (Gal 2:19-20). Within the Christian tradition, the Quakers have talked for the past few centuries of seeing "that of God in everyone".

John's Gospel (John 1:18) says, "No one has ever seen God" and then goes on to say that God the Son has revealed him. However, in the first Epistle (1 John 4:12) the same statement is made, but this time followed up with "if we love one another, God lives in us". Here we have the suggestion that God is not some being who meets us from outside, but that where there is love between human beings God is present.

At the same time we cannot get away from the prevailing sense in the Bible that God is a person. This is perhaps the most fundamental difference between the God of the Bible and the ethos of much present-day spirituality. The God of the Bible is spirit (John 4:24), but not *just* spirit. Though the Bible writers acknowledge the presence of God in everything, they do not see God simply as an impersonal force or universal principle: God is a person, someone with whom human beings have a relationship.

A relationship with a real person has its ups and downs. Things go wrong, misunderstandings happen, there are quarrels, people are hurt, they fall out with each other and have to be reconciled. For the Bible writers, the good news is not that everything is perfect if only we can see it that way. The good news is that, however much we have hurt God, God still loves us and is willing to forgive us.

Western culture has imbibed this Judaeo-Christian type of spirituality. God is someone we pray to, someone we can obey or disobey, someone we question and argue with, someone with whom we can have the kind of relationship children have with their parents, both loving and rebelling. When we suffer we often instinctively ask "Why is God doing this to me?" We do not feel we can pin responsibility for what happens in the world on some essence that is not a person, nor can we see it as simply an emanation of ourselves. In Western culture, even among people who do not believe in God, there is often a preoccupation with the question of whether life is "fair". Even without believing in God, many people somehow feel the need to question the order of the universe *as if* someone was in charge of it.

The first Letter of John takes a further step in exploring the nature of God, coming up with the simple bold statement that "God is love". It is expressed both negatively and positively:

"Whoever does not love does not know God, for God is love" (1 John 4:8), and "God is love, and those who abide in love abide in God, and God abides in them" (1 John 4:16). This resonates with the feeling of many people today that it is hard to believe in or imagine God as a *person*, but that the *experience* of God is nevertheless very real.

However, if we define God as love we cannot get away from the personal. To say that God is "light", as the same Epistle does at another point (1 John 1:5) leaves open the possibility that there is no personal God, since light is an impersonal thing. Love, on the other hand, is something that happens between persons, and it cannot exist without a person. It seems that what some parts of the Bible are striving towards in this kind of apparently abstract statement is that God is not "a person" as such, but is personal. If God is a force, spirit or principle, this makes God *less* than a person. What some of the Bible writers are trying to express, and what the Christian doctrine of the Trinity is trying to express, is that God is *more* than a person.

Notes

1. "Sheol" is the Hebrew word for the world of the dead, the underworld.

5

Looking for Meaning

"things that we have heard and known, that our ancestors have told us"
(Ps 78:3)

Stories are central to human life. Most of us make sure we never miss the daily news on television or in the papers. We may tell ourselves that this is our duty as responsible citizens, but the real motive is more basic. Human beings have an insatiable hunger for stories. We are always exchanging the latest gossip about our friends and neighbours. Whenever we meet someone we "catch up" on the things that have happened since the last time we met, whether it was years ago or just earlier the same day. When we have a leisurely conversation over dinner with friends, or get into a long chat with someone we have just met, the conversation usually revolves around the story of our lives: childhood experiences, jobs we have had, places where we have lived, memorable people we have known, holidays, illnesses, strange coincidences, amusing incidents and so on.

When we run short of true stories we turn to invented ones. The voracious appetite of many people today for films and novels and the avid way in which they follow the ups and downs of characters in the television soap operas is only a modern manifestation of a perennial characteristic of human life. In every human culture story-telling has had its place alongside sport, music and dancing as a standard way of spending leisure hours.

It is by telling stories that we give shape and meaning to our lives. When we have a particularly traumatic experience we find great relief in simply talking about it, telling the whole story in detail to anyone willing to listen. This is our way of coming to terms with the experience emotionally, regaining equilibrium, digesting this new "foreign body" into our consciousness so that we can live with it.

Stories also help us to understand ourselves. We look back over our lives to get insight into where we have come from and a clearer idea of where we may be going. People who are discontented with their lives sometimes talk of having "lost the plot". We have an instinctive feeling that our life should be a story with a beginning, a line of development and a satisfactory ending. Our stories tell us who we are. Much of the process of getting to know people is a matter of listening to their stories.

The Bible is full of stories. They are not just there "for the record", or simply to satisfy the curiosity of historians. They are part of the process of a people seeking to understand their world and themselves.

Some of the early stories are attempts to answer questions human beings have always asked. How did the world start? Why does the earth produce weeds and poisonous plants? Why do we die? Why do human beings wear clothes? Why do women have pain in childbirth? Why are there different languages? The ancestors of the Jews shared stories like these with surrounding cultures. Sometimes they would pick up a story from another culture and re-shape it in the light of their distinctive faith. These are not simply "just so" stories. They are attempts to understand the world in the light of a distinctive conception of God. The creation story with which the Bible begins has probably borrowed motifs from the creation myths of other cultures, but as it now stands it is a confident assertion of belief in one God.

This is also true of the story of Noah and the flood. It has striking similarities with a story in the Mesopotamian Epic of Gilgamesh, which dates from some time before 2000 BCE, but the differences too are just as striking. In that story the god Enlil urges the other gods to destroy human beings, not because of their sin but simply because he is irritated – they have become so numerous that he cannot sleep for the noise they are making! Another god, Ea, warns one man, Utnapishtim, of their intention, apparently not for any reason except that he favours him. He gives him detailed instructions for the building of a boat to save himself, his family and "the seed of every living thing". After the flood, as in the biblical story, Utnapishtim sends birds out to ascertain whether the waters have receded. When the boat comes to rest on dry land and he offers up a sacrifice, the gods smell the sweet savour and gather "like flies" around it. They then lament what has happened, and a quarrel breaks out. Enlil is angry that his order has been disobeyed and one human family has survived, but the other gods are angry with him for causing this senseless destruction.

The similarities make it quite obvious that this story is not unique to the Bible. What is unique is what the Bible makes of it. In the biblical flood story there are no competing and quarrelling gods, just one God in charge of everything. He resolves to destroy the human race because it is not living according to his moral standards, but spares Noah because he is "a righteous man, blameless in his generation" (Gen 6:9). When the flood is over, that same God smells the sacrifice and expresses his own regret, making a solemn promise never to do such a thing again. And so this primitive story that once involved many gods has been re-moulded to express the faith of Israel in one God who acts from ethical principles rather than passing whims.

Making Sense of Israel's History

After these primeval stories, the Book of Genesis starts telling the story of one particular people. God calls Abram (later re-named Abraham) to leave his family home and heritage behind and move to a new country. He promises him that, though he is old and has no children yet, he will have innumerable descendants and they will occupy the land to which he is moving. Miraculously, his wife Sarah has a son in her old age. The family history is then traced through that son, Isaac, Isaac's son Jacob, and Jacob's twelve sons who are the ancestors of the twelve tribes of Israel. One of them, Joseph, is hated by his brothers. They seize him and sell him as a slave. He is taken to Egypt, where after many years he becomes a powerful leader, second only to Pharaoh. In a time of famine, the other sons of Jacob come to Egypt to buy grain, and eventually Joseph is reconciled with them, and the whole family is allowed to settle in Egypt in order to escape the famine.

Some generations go by, and Jacob's descendants, now called "the children of Israel", "Israelites" or "Hebrews", have multiplied, but have become an oppressed slave community in Egypt. God calls Moses to organize their escape and leads them through the desert to the land that he had promised to Abraham. After years of wandering in the desert, the children of these slaves enter the Promised Land and conquer it. At first they are a league of tribes led from time to time by charismatic leaders, but eventually they appoint Saul as a king. He is displaced by David, who establishes his capital in Jerusalem, where his descendants reign in an unbroken dynasty for more than four hundred years. David's successor is his son Solomon, a king of legendary wealth and wisdom. However, after Solomon's death there is a revolt, and the kingdom splits into two, Israel in the north and Judah in the south. After about two hundred years Israel falls to the Assyrian Empire, and Judah continues alone for another hundred and thirty years before falling to the Babylonians, who destroy Jerusalem and deport most of its leading citizens to Babylon.

This is the story of ancient Israel as the Bible tells it. Scholars differ as to how much of it is historically accurate, but one thing we cannot doubt is how remarkable it is that the story was told at all. The history of the kingdoms of Israel and Judah was a comparatively brief one, and their significance on the world stage was never very great. Judah was just one of a number of small kingdoms overrun by the Babylonians and absorbed into their empire. However, while most of the others permanently disappeared from the map, the Jewish nation survived. Today, more than two thousand five hundred years later, the Jews still exist as a people, there is a state of Israel, and Jerusalem is not only a holy city for three religions but also an evocative spiritual image. For Christians, "Zion, city of our God" is symbolic of the church, "Jerusalem the golden" is an image of Heaven, and the ultimate ideal world is called "the new Jerusalem". All this has happened because of the peculiar nature of the faith of the Jews.

The Jews believed that God had chosen them to be his holy people. He had given them laws and made them witnesses to himself as the one, righteous God. He had given them the land of Canaan. He had designated the city of Jerusalem as his dwelling place, the city of which one of the psalms says: "God is in the midst of her; she shall not be moved" (Ps 46:5). He had made a covenant with David, promising him an eternal dynasty. And so the conquest by the Babylonians was not just a political disaster but a blow to basic tenets of their faith. The sacred monarchy was abolished, the holy city and its Temple were destroyed, and most of the leading citizens were taken away from the Promised Land. At the same time, that faith was so strong and so deeply ingrained in some of the people that they were determined to hold on to it in spite of everything that had happened. In the depths of defeat the people of Judah kept their identity by telling and re-telling their story and trying to make sense of it. They had to find meaning in the failures as well as the successes.

In order to do this, they drew on the ancient stories of Abraham, Isaac and Jacob, reinforcing their belief that God had some special purpose for their nation from the very beginning. They also reflected on their history to ask why God had blessed the people in earlier days and why that blessing had been withdrawn. From this reflection a pattern emerged. In the days before there was a kingdom they had fallen into the hands of their enemies whenever they forgot their own God and turned to other gods, but when they prayed to God he took pity on them and raised up a leader to rally them and overcome the enemy (Judg 2:11-23). Later, when they were ruled by kings, the same pattern of judgment and restoration continued. When the king and the nation were faithful to God there was peace and prosperity, but when the king led the people into idolatry and injustice disaster soon followed. However, the God who judged and punished could also forgive. If the people repented of their sins and purified their life he would again turn to them with his favour, remember his promise to Abraham, Isaac and Jacob, and restore them. This was the hope that sustained them in the Babylonian Exile and all the hardships that followed it.

The telling of this story was deeply influenced by a succession of remarkable people known as the "prophets". These were not primarily predictors of the future (the popular meaning of "prophet" today) but interpreters of their own time. Whatever the *history*, it was largely the prophets who made the *story*: or rather, some of the prophets. The idea of a prophet in ancient Israel, as in other cultures, seems to have originated from the "seer" or clairvoyant, and of the spell-binder, the one who could speak a powerful word to make things happen. The early kings had prophets to whom they would turn either for guidance when there was a decision to be made or for a blessing on their armies and a curse on their enemies when they went to war. However, it seems that from quite early times some at least of the prophets were not content simply to boost the king's confidence or help the nation to win battles. They were campaigners for the true worship of the God of Israel, standing up and rebuking the rulers, and acting as the conscience of the nation. They were probably a minority in their time, and labelled as trouble-makers, but their words have survived in the Bible while most of the more acceptable official prophets have been forgotten.

The archetypal prophet was Elijah. Dramatic stories were told of how he had confronted King Ahab and his idol-worshipping queen Jezebel. Ahab called him "you troubler of Israel" (1 Kgs 18:17). Jezebel threatened to kill him (1 Kgs 19:2). Elijah was succeeded by his disciple Elisha, who also played a great part in the political life of the time, including the coup that overthrew Ahab's family and resulted in the gruesome death of Jezebel (2 Kgs 10:30-37).

One of the most unpopular prophets in his lifetime was Jeremiah. He lived in the last days of the kingdom of Judah, and saw its destruction by the Babylonians. In the years leading up to this, most of the prophets were doing the job they had always done, trying to boost the morale of the people by assuring them that God would never allow his holy city to be conquered. But Jeremiah said of them: "They have treated the wound of my people carelessly, saying, 'Peace, peace', when there is no peace." (Jer 6:14). Jeremiah stuck firmly to his belief that the nation enjoyed the favour and protection of God because of its nature as a holy people, and when it forsook that nature it no longer had any right to protection. In his view even the Temple in Jerusalem, that was thought to be the very dwelling place of God, was not guaranteed. One day he stood at the entrance of the Temple and addressed the people as they were going in to worship. We can almost hear his mocking tone as he repeated the mantra that made them feel safe:

"Do not trust in these deceptive words: 'This is the temple of the LORD, the temple of the LORD, the temple of the LORD'... Will you steal, murder, commit adultery, swear falsely, make offerings to Baal, and go after other gods that you have not known, and then come and stand before me in this house, which is called by my name, and say 'We are safe!'... Has this house become a den of robbers in your sight?" (Jer 7:4-11)

Later, as the Babylonian army was laying siege to Jerusalem,

Jeremiah, rather than boosting the morale of the people, was exhorting them to surrender (Jer 21:8-10). A few years after that, when many Jews had been taken into exile in Babylon, Jeremiah sent them a letter encouraging them to settle there, not to rebel but to seek the welfare of Babylon and pray for it, because this was all part of God's judgment and at the same time God's loving long-term purpose for them (Jer 29).

The prophets, then, were in part foreseers of the future, but this was because they had a clear understanding of what was going on in their own time and a sense of morality that convinced them that injustice and unfaithfulness to God had inevitable consequences. They were not so much clairvoyants as visionaries. Most of their words are in poetic form. Like many poets they are sometimes a bit difficult to understand, and when we do understand them they often offer a disturbing perspective on life and society. Because they look beneath the surface and see things most people do not notice, they are often ahead of their time.

The words of the prophets whose predictions proved true were repeated and eventually preserved in writing, often adapted for new circumstances where they seemed equally relevant. It was under the influence of their interpretation of events that the whole story of the kingdoms of Israel and Judah was written up in the books of Samuel and Kings, with its preamble in Joshua and Judges and a revision of the older stories and laws in the books from Genesis to Deuteronomy. This makes it entirely appropriate that in the Jewish Bible the books from Joshua to Kings are included in the category of "the Prophets": the whole history is shot through with prophetic interpretation. It is not "history" in the modern sense of the word, but a kind of sermon on the ways of God with his people.

This focus on history and its meaning is a distinctive mark of the biblical faith. Many religious traditions have little relationship with history. They are bound up with the cycle of the seasons – rites surrounding ploughing, sowing and harvest, celebrating mid-summer and mid-winter and so on. For them, one year is much the same as another. Other traditions, including most of the popular kinds of spirituality today, concentrate on the individual soul and its eternal destiny. Christianity too, both in its Catholic and in its evangelical forms, has mostly tended to focus on the salvation of the soul and its ultimate destination of Heaven or Hell. Even those who assert a literal interpretation of the "second coming" of Christ see it in terms of the final judgment of every individual. They see specific political events as fulfilment of prophecy and signs that "the end is near", but they do not view the whole of history as a meaningful process working towards a goal. For them the end of the world is a sudden termination of whatever is happening, like switching off the television in the middle of a programme. While there are elements of all this in the Bible, the biblical faith generally is an ongoing interpretation of history. It sees God at work not just in the lives of individuals, and certainly not just in their "spiritual" lives, but in the events of history and their effect on whole nations and communities. Many Christians today are finding that a faith like this inspires us not to cultivate our own spiritual progress but to live wholeheartedly in the world as members of society committed to justice and peace.

More than One Story

The Jews' interpretation of their story was not unanimous. There were alternative stories – what we might call minority reports.

Concerning the monarchy, for instance, there is more than one picture. In many parts of the scriptures it is regarded as a divinely ordained institution. The story (2 Sam 7) is that when David had settled in his palace in Jerusalem he determined to build a temple to house the sacred Ark of God which had hitherto only been covered by a tent. However, he received a message from God through the prophet Nathan that he was not to be the one to build a temple: that would be a task for his son. Instead of David giving God a house, God would give David a "house", that is a dynasty, which would last for ever. This is celebrated in several of the psalms, which probably reflect coronations, or occasions when the king presided over acts of worship. God says, "I have set my king on Zion, my holy hill... You are my son, today I have begotten you. Ask of me, and I will make the nations your heritage, and the ends of the earth your possession" (Ps 2:6-8). The king is called "the firstborn, the highest of the kings of the earth" (Ps 89:27).

At times when things were not going well for the nation, hopes for a better future were often centred on a king whom God would bless. The prophet Isaiah rejoices in the birth of a child in the royal family with words familiar to many from Christmas carol services: "For unto us a child is born, unto us a son is given... Of the increase of his government and peace there shall be no end, upon the throne of David, and upon his kingdom, to order it, and to establish it with judgment and with justice from henceforth even forever" (Is 9:6-7, AV). A little further on is another vision of an ideal king, this time called "a shoot from the stock of Jesse" (Is 11:1). Jesse was David's father, and it looks as if the prophet meant that even if the whole line of David was wiped out God would start again.

After Jerusalem had fallen to the Babylonians and the monarchy was no more, there were still visions of a future king. Zechariah says: "Lo, your king comes to you; triumphant and victorious is he, humble and riding on a donkey" (Zech 9:9). By the time of Jesus this had become the expectation of the Messiah, God's Anointed, the Son of David, who would save the nation. The angel Gabriel, telling Mary of the birth of her son, says: "the Lord God will give to him the throne of his ancestor David. He will reign over the house of Jacob forever, and of his kingdom there will be no end" (Luke 1:32-33). The name "Christ" is the Greek equivalent of "Messiah", the Anointed One, and so the

Christian faith itself derives its name from this ancient Israelite image of monarchy.

But there is another story (1 Sam 8) that presents a very different picture. It says that the people approached their aged and respected leader Samuel and urged him to appoint "a king to govern us, like other nations". Samuel was disturbed about this and prayed about it. God's response was to say: "they have not rejected you, but they have rejected me from being king over them". The demand to have a king "like other nations" was a denial of Israel's calling to be a special, unique people under the rule of God. God allowed them to go ahead with it, but told Samuel that he should "solemnly warn them, and show them the ways of the king who shall reign over them". Samuel duly did this, warning them that a king would conscript their sons to be his horsemen, to plough his fields and manufacture his weapons, would make their daughters his cooks, would take over their land and demand tithes of them to enrich his favourites, and so on, and that one day "you will cry out because of your king, whom you have chosen for yourselves; but the LORD will not answer you in that day" (1 Sam 8:18).

The Book of Deuteronomy (17:14-20) is also rather ambivalent about kingship. It permits the people to appoint a king, but he must not acquire too many horses, too much wealth or too many wives. This is a fairly obvious reference to Solomon. In fact it specifically says that the king should not acquire horses from Egypt, the very thing Solomon is said to have done (1 Kgs 10: 28-29).

There was clearly an ongoing debate about kingship, perhaps not in the heyday of the dynasty of David, but some time later when the preaching of the prophets had begun to expose the dangers of idolatry, and perhaps especially after the Exile, when there was controversy as to whether the monarchy should be restored. Some wrote the history in a way that showed how good kings brought blessing while idolatrous and disobedient kings brought disaster on the nation, but others went further and suggested that the very existence of a monarchy was a bad idea from the start. The side of the debate that favoured monarchy is strongly represented in the books of Chronicles which, unlike Samuel and Kings, make no reference to the people's request for a king and Samuel's response to it, and have nothing negative to say about the reign of Solomon. The account of Solomon's wealth and power in Chronicles closely follows the one in Kings, but omits the reference to the huge number of his foreign wives and the way in which they drew him into idolatry (1 Kgs 10:14-29; 2 Chr 9:13-28).

It is remarkable that these anti-monarchic passages have survived, along with the proud descriptions of Solomon's reign and the high theology of kingship in the psalms, as part of the same Bible. There must have been a deep division of opinion, yet writings representing both points of view were copied and preserved. The people who produced the Bible were not like modern authors or editors: they were simply faithful compilers, tending to preserve anything ancient that was available. They may even have been aware that the issue of monarchy was still in their time a controversial one, and decided to represent more than one side of the debate. As we read the Bible today, there is no point in trying to reconcile all these different accounts and try to make one consistent story of them. What we have in the Hebrew scriptures is an ongoing debate in which many voices speak, each telling their own story for their own purpose.

There is a sense in which the debate continues to this day. The association of kingship with the Christian faith, talk of "Christ the King" and so on, has become a problematic issue in our time. The concept of "the Kingdom of Heaven" was also a key feature in the teaching of Jesus. Some people are suggesting today that some of this imagery needs to be questioned and revised. Calling Jesus "Lord" or "King" not only stresses his masculinity rather than his universal meaning for humanity, it also reflects a world that is rapidly disappearing. Most nations today do not have a king or queen or titles such as "Lord". The ideal to which we all aspire is democracy. Should we think more of Jesus as our charismatic Leader, and talk of "the Republic of Heaven"? Such suggestions may seem shocking to many Christians, but perhaps would not have been so shocking to that minority of Bible writers who were questioning the whole institution of monarchy more than two thousand years ago.

Another example of this telling of a different story is the Book of Ruth. The way in which the historians interpreted the nation's misfortunes as a judgment on its idolatry and its lax attitude to mingling with other peoples led to an extreme emphasis on purity and separation. After some of the Jews had returned from exile Ezra was dismayed to find that many had intermarried with the other nations in the land, and he took extremely strict measures to preserve the purity of the Jewish community, demanding that those who were married to non-Jews turn their wives and children out (Ezra 9-10). It may be from this time that we should date the extreme intolerance displayed in the Book of Deuteronomy, where the Israelites entering the Promised Land are instructed to destroy all the inhabitants without mercy in case they should be tempted to join them in the worship of their gods (Deut 7:1-6). One of the psalms deplores the fact that this commandment was not obeyed (Ps 106:34-35).

The Book of Ruth, however, tells the story of how, back in the days before the monarchy, a Judean couple emigrated to the land of the Moabites, and how their two sons married Moabite women (a sin according to the law in Deut 23:3). The husband died, and so did his two sons (a judgment for their sin, some would say). But it then goes on to tell how one of the daughters-in-law, Ruth, determined to stay with her late husband's mother and support her. She accompanied her back to Judah and went out gleaning in the fields in order to help them both to survive. This came to the attention of Boaz, the landowner, who turned out to be a near kinsman of Naomi's husband. There was a custom of levirate marriage, by which if a man dies without children his next of kin should marry the widow and raise children in his name. Since Naomi was probably too old to bear children by that time, Boaz married Ruth, so committing the "sin" of marrying a Moabite. But far from being cursed, this marriage was richly blessed. The great King David himself was their great-grandson.

The Book of Ecclesiastes, or "the Preacher", presents an even greater challenge to the interpretation of the story. The words in its title, "the son of David, king in Jerusalem", imply that Solomon is supposed to be the author, but much of what it says seems to breathe the spirit of a much later age. It begins with a saying that is one of the most familiar in the Bible. In the King James Version it says: "Vanity of vanities, saith the Preacher, vanity of vanities; all is vanity". This word has been variously interpreted. It obviously does not refer to vanity in the usual modern sense of the word, but is nearer to the meaning of "vain" as in the expression "in vain". It suggests emptiness, point-lessness, futility. The Good News Bible translates it as "It is useless... all useless". The New International Version uses the word "meaningless". Ecclesiastes reflects on the ephemeral nature of human life. However hard we work, however much we achieve, we will die. However famous we may be, the time will come when we are forgotten. Even people not yet born will one day be forgotten, as if they had never lived (Eccles 1:11). Even if we seek the higher values like wisdom rather than just wealth and pleasure, we are no better off, because the wise die as well as the foolish (Eccles 2:14). Human beings are only animals, destined to return to the earth from which they came: how can we know whether our ultimate destiny is different from that of any other animal (Eccles 3:19-21)?

The writer seems to be denying the possibility of any inter-pretation of history: "A generation goes, and a generation comes, but the earth remains for ever... What has been is what will be, and what has been done is what will be done; there is nothing new under the sun" (Eccles 1:4,9). These are sentiments more characteristic of an atheist or an agnostic than of a religious believer. The quest for meaning has reached the point of questioning whether there is any meaning at all. Again, we are reminded that the Bible is not a manual of straightforward teaching, but an ongoing debate. If we take the search for meaning seriously, we may be inspired by a grand vision of God working through history, but at the same time we are challenged to grapple with the issues raised in books like Ecclesiastes.

Is the Story True?

The story the Bible tells is a complex web of stories rather than one consistent, straightforward narrative. The people who formed the Bible we now have were repeating stories they had heard or read and at the same time re-working them, re-shaping them, and putting them together in new combinations.

If we are looking for consistency, we will find it challenged on almost every page. One of the earliest examples is the old heckler's question: "Who was Cain's wife?" The traditional interpretation of Genesis has been that Adam and Eve were the first human beings and we are all descended from them. But when one of their sons murdered the other, who was left? The story says that Cain went off to another country, married and had children. It even says that he built a city and named it after his son Enoch. Where did all these people come from?

A little further on there is another inconsistency that is not so often noticed. The logic of the story in Genesis is that not only are we all descended from Adam and Eve, but since the whole human race was destroyed in the flood except Noah and his wife and sons, we are also all descended from Noah. However, before mentioning Noah the Bible tells us that among the descendants of Cain were Jabal, "the ancestor of those who live in tents and have livestock", and Jubal, "the ancestor of all those who play the lyre and pipe" (Gen 4:20-21). But if all except Noah and his family died in the flood, how can distinct groups of people be descended from ancestors who lived before Noah? It looks as if these references to Cain and his descendants are part of a collection of stories that were once quite separate from the Adam and Eve story. The whole account of the descendants of Cain (Gen 4:17-24), ending with an extremely cryptic saying of Lamech to his wives, seems in fact to be a kind of dead end, with no connection with the main plot. It was evidently included in the Book of Genesis just because it was an old story.

Inconsistencies like this abound in the Hebrew scriptures. The story of Noah and the flood (Gen 6-9), apart from being physically impossible, shows the marks of at least two stories woven together. The number of creatures taken into the ark is not clear (one pair or seven?), nor is the chronology (compare Gen 6:19; 7:2-3, 8-9, 11; 8:6-12, 13-14). What seems to have happened it that the compilers knew two different versions of the story, and so took one of them and supplemented it with details from the other worked in at the appropriate points. A similar thing seems to have happened with the story of the ten plagues by which Pharaoh was persuaded to let the Hebrew slaves go (Ex 7-13). It is an untidy story in which the pattern keeps changing. Sometimes Aaron brings on a plague by using his staff, but at other times Moses is the initiator and Aaron is not in the picture at all. If we take it as one literal account, it seems that all the cattle in Egypt died three times! Here too there seem to be at least two different stories woven together. There are also slightly different accounts of the plagues in two of the psalms (Ps 78:44-51; 105:28-36).

To take just one more example: how did David first become associated with King Saul? We are told (1 Sam 16:14-23) that Saul was having bouts of mental illness or, as the text puts it "an evil spirit from the LORD tormented him". His servants went looking for a skilled player of the lyre who could soothe him, and they found David. Saul took a great liking to David, and as well as benefiting from his musical ability he made him his armour-bearer. In the next chapter, however, we have the famous story of David and Goliath. In this story we are introduced to David "the son of an Ephrathite of Bethlehem in Judah" (1 Sam 17:12) as if we had not heard of him before. The story then goes on to tell how David came to bring food to his soldier brothers, heard about Goliath's challenge to the Israelites for someone to take him on in single combat, and volunteered to take it up. This was brought to the attention of Saul, who after some hesitation accepted David's offer. He put his armour on David, but David rejected it and killed Goliath just with one stone from his own sling. But then at the end of the story (1 Sam 17:55-58) we find Saul asking Abner, the commander of his army, "whose son is this young man?" Abner does not know, so they call David so that Saul can find out who he is. Yet another inconsistency appears further on (2 Sam 21:19) in a passage about some of the heroic exploits during David's reign. Here we are told of a giant from Gath called Goliath, "the shaft of whose spear was like a weaver's beam", the very words used of the Goliath whom David killed (1 Sam 17:7). This man was killed by Elhanan who, like David, came from Bethlehem. It looks very much as if a story originally told of Elhanan was transferred to the much more famous David.

The reason for inconsistencies like these could be that the stories to which the editors had access were all both ancient and revered, so that they did not feel free to select one and neglect others. On the other hand, the editors may have seen the stories as having different points, or showing different aspects of the situation, and deliberately kept both versions. Such a procedure was more generally acceptable in that culture than it is in ours, though in fact some modern novels and films employ a similar technique. They tell the story several times from the point of view of different characters, or explore what the long term consequences would have been if one little thing had turned out differently. It is evident in many parts of the Bible that the point being made was regarded as more important than historical accuracy or consistency.

Critical study of the Bible has often concentrated on the attempt to reconstruct the history. Being creatures of our time, we feel obliged to do this. We cannot pretend that facts and history are unimportant. The critical mindset, the habit of thinking rationally and scientifically, is built into us by our culture and education. If we try to bypass the critical approach there are traps we can fall into. We can find ourselves defending beliefs that are quite frankly ridiculous, or struggling to reconcile obvious contradictions. Worse still, we can end up trying to justify inhumane laws, or some of the appalling behaviour that the Bible says God approved of or even commanded. For reasons like this it is important to distinguish between what may have actually happened and what the writers made of it: to recognize exaggerations, embellishments and (most important) interpretations we may not agree with.

However, scholars today are turning more and more to the appreciation of the Bible as a book of stories. It is not *what actually happened* that really matters, but *the story being told*. If we are too obsessed with what "really" happened, we are treating the Bible as a history text book. This only serves to draw attention to its inaccuracy and incompleteness, and to give ammunition to atheist critics. But the biblical stories were never meant to be a history text book. They were meant to inspire their readers by telling the story of God's dealings with his people. The Bible is a book of stories with a message or, if you like, of statements of faith backed up by stories. As we read, we need to feel the feelings of those who gave us the story as it now is, to appreciate why they are telling it, and to allow ourselves to be moved by it. Paradoxically, this means reading the Bible *uncritically*: not in the sense of thinking "this is what actually happened", but in the sense of being non-judgmental. As we read we remember that this story comes out of the experience of other human beings, and as such it is valid and interesting. We are not obliged to agree or disagree with it: we can just read it.

What are Stories For?

In our everyday life we tell stories for different purposes. Some have immediate practical implications. Perhaps you are about to buy a fairly expensive item, and someone tells you how they got it much cheaper somewhere else. Or perhaps a friend is warning you that someone you are thinking of doing business with has let them down badly in the past. These are stories with practical implications, and it is important to know whether or not they are factual. The question of accuracy will directly affect your own actions.

At the other extreme are the stories we tell one another purely for entertainment and amusement. If someone tells you a joke, or relates some amusing experience, it really doesn't matter whether the story is true, exaggerated or just made up. Its main purpose is to make you laugh, and if it does that it has achieved its purpose. Only a boring spoilsport would insist on cross-examining the story-teller to ascertain what "really" happened.

There are also stories, like Aesop's Fables or the parables of Jesus, which are obviously made up to make a point. With these, too, it would be foolish to ask for more detailed information about characters, dates and so on or to enquire into the accuracy of the story.

On a different level again are the serious personal stories in which people share their life experience and disclose something important about themselves. If someone is telling us that kind of story, it will affect us in a personal way. We may find that it resonates so much with our own experience that we feel we have made a new friend. Or the opposite may happen: we may be repelled or puzzled and think "I really don't like this person".

Listening to someone whose life is totally different from our own may make a difference to the way we ourselves see the world from that moment on. Whether we end up warming to the story, reacting against it, or suspending judgment, we have changed and grown as people simply by *listening* to someone else's story. This is the sort of thing that can happen when we read the Bible. In some stories we may find a kindred spirit. Other stories may repel us, and others again may provoke us into thinking in a new way.

When someone is telling you something that is very important to them you try to give them your undivided attention. You do not interrupt by asking awkward questions or demanding irrelevant information. The person is telling you the story they want to tell. They are including what is important to them, passing over what is not important to them, and putting their own interpretation on the events. Respect for that person prompts you simply to listen and try to understand why they are telling you that story. The time may come when you have to check the facts or question their interpretation of what happened, but initially the important thing is to listen. This person is telling you the story in order that you may understand them better as a person. What really matters is not the detail, or even how accurate their memory is. What matters is what the story means to them *now*, how it has made them who they are.

Many of the stories in the Bible are of that kind. People are telling their story – the story that explains how they tick, who they think they are and why. They are in a sense defining themselves. The writers of the Hebrew scriptures believed that the God who created the whole world had somehow dealt with their nation in a special way. He had chosen them for a purpose. He had helped them, set them free, guided them, rebuked, judged and forgiven them down through the generations. This is the faith of Jewish people to this day, and it has made them who they are. The people who wrote the New Testament believed that this same God had revealed himself in a special way in Jesus of Nazareth: that Jesus had taught us to trust in God and to love one another, that he had been condemned to death but was alive for ever, and that his death and Resurrection were cosmic events defining God's relationship with humanity. This too is what makes Christians who they are to this day. What matters is not the dates and times, nor the accuracy of the history, but the fact that this is the story that we people of faith tell about our God and ourselves. It is the story by which we define ourselves and by which we seek to make sense of our experience.

Many of the Bible stories are told in different versions. The Book of Deuteronomy recapitulates the story of the Exodus as a sermon in which Moses reminds the people of what God has done for them and what he expects of them. The whole story from Genesis through to 2 Kings is re-told with a different slant in 1 and 2 Chronicles. In the New Testament the story of Jesus is told four times, and there are differences in the telling. It is as if the Bible is constantly supplementing, adapting, correcting and updating its own story. This too points to something very important about the Bible and the communities that created it. As time goes by we all see past events from a different perspective. Sometimes even our memory of them gradually changes: we remember events through the filter of what they mean to us now, and are quite convinced that what we now remember corresponds to what actually happened. The communities behind the Bible were story-telling communities, and this meant that they were also story-*changing* communities. The function of their stories was to help them define who they were, and this inevitably meant that as their identity and circumstances changed so did their stories.

We, with our modern mentality, sometimes find it hard to understand how people could relate "historical" events while knowingly altering them, but we cannot escape the fact that this happened. Changes in interpreting the *significance* of events are quite understandable. We can perhaps appreciate that one writer could say that God in his anger incited David to the sin of counting the people (2 Sam 24), while another could say it was the work of Satan (1 Chr 21). But changing the *facts* seems a different thing to us. We have to recognize here that the mindset of the ancient world was not the same as ours. People in those days thought symbolically and mythically, and sometimes the facts were less important to them than the meaning. If the story was edifying and inspiring, it did not greatly matter whether it was factually accurate.

Fiction in the name of religion is not entirely unknown even in modern times. Every Christmas the stories of the birth of Jesus are routinely adapted to make a nativity play, with a stable full of cattle and three crowned kings appearing at the same time as the shepherds. Films about the life of Jesus always include things that are not mentioned in the Gospels, or tell the Gospel stories in a different way and a different order. We usually find this kind of thing quite acceptable. Not quite so excusable perhaps, but very prevalent, is the behaviour of those Christian preachers who accept biblical criticism in their studies but pretend to believe the stories literally when they are in the pulpit.

With all the biblical stories we can only suspend judgment and recognize that this was *the story the writers wanted to tell*, and that the question we should be asking is not what really happened but why telling the story in this way was so important to them.

6

The Cry for Help

"How long, O LORD?"
(Ps 13:1-2; 35:17; 79:5; etc.)

"God is an unutterable sigh, lying in the depths of the soul"
(Jean Paul Richter)

The simplest, most basic quest for God happens when people are in desperate trouble and cry out in prayer. Of all the books in the Bible, the Book of Psalms is the one that supremely expresses this. Its popularity lies to a great extent in the fact that people in all kinds of situations can identify with its prayers.

We may take just one psalm (Ps 38) as an example. It begins: "O LORD, do not rebuke me in your anger, or discipline me in your wrath. For your arrows have sunk into me, and your hand has come down on me". Here we immediately find the directness and bluntness of so much of the praying of the people behind the Bible. People today tend to put the questions to someone else *about* God: "Why does God allow this to happen? What have I done to deserve it?" The people of the Bible tended to put the questions directly *to* God. They assumed that God was in charge, so that whatever happened, good or bad, it was God who was doing it. They often also assumed that suffering was a punishment for sin. The person saying this prayer is physically ill – "There is no soundness in my flesh... there is no health in my bones... My wounds grow foul and fester". Whatever the illness, it affects his whole body including his eyesight – "as for the light of my eyes – it also has gone from me". He notices how people shun him, unable to cope with such suffering, or perhaps because they too condemn him: "My friends and companions stand aloof from my affliction, and my neighbours stand far off". Even worse, there are enemies who are apparently using his affliction to their own advantage: "Those who seek my life lay their snares; those who seek to hurt me speak of ruin, and meditate treachery all day long". In all this, he throws himself upon the mercy of God, and ends the prayer with an urgent plea: "make haste to help me, O Lord, my salvation". In spite of some cultural differences, and perhaps a view of divine punishment that we find difficult today, there is something universally human about a prayer like this. It is suggestive of the plight of many people today who suffer with a disease that carries a stigma, such as Aids or leprosy in some parts of the world.

The people of the Bible had a strong feeling that God heard the cry of those in distress. Often the sign of injustice, and the first step towards justice being done, is a cry for help. Isaiah employs a striking play on words as he talks of God looking to Israel for justice (*tsedaqah*) but finding a cry (*tse'aqah*), for righteousness (*mishpat*) but finding cries of distress (*mishpach*) (Is 5:7). We read that when the Hebrew slaves in Egypt were cruelly treated by their slave-masters, "their cry for help rose up to God", and he said to Moses, "I have come down to deliver them from the Egyptians" (Ex 2:23; 3:8). In the commandments the people are warned not to abuse a widow or an orphan, because, says God, "when they cry out to me, I will surely heed their cry" (Ex 22:23; cf. v27, etc.). Even a dead body could be a cry: near the beginning of the Bible, when Cain murders his brother Abel, God confronts him and says "What have you done? Listen; your brother's blood is crying out to me from the ground!" (Gen 4:10).

The cry to God for help is a universal human experience, but so is the experience that it is often ineffective. We are left wondering whether there really is a God who hears our prayers. In our modern way of thinking, even when prayers seem to be answered we are sceptical. "Miracles" are hard to believe in, and we prefer to explain things in terms of the influence of the mind over the body, the power of suggestion or of positive thinking, and so on. Symptoms even of a serious disease can sometimes disappear in unpredictable ways. It has to be acknowledged too that in a world of almost infinite possibility the most remarkable coincidences, such as someone getting exactly what they pray for at the time they pray for it, are bound to happen *some* time. Even many people who pray regularly do not believe that God literally gives them what they ask for. They value prayer for the influence it has on their own attitudes, or the comfort it gives to people who know they are being prayed for, not because they believe it can actually change the state of anyone's internal organs, much less change the weather. And added to all this is the experience of the many people who pray desperately for healing, for protection or for rescue, and nevertheless suffer and die.

For the people of the Bible the question about prayer was not, as it often is for us, whether God exists – that was rarely if ever doubted. The question was whether God is taking any notice of our prayers. Jesus, in one of his parables (Luke 11:5-8), compares prayer to knocking on a friend's door at midnight to borrow bread for an unexpected visitor. The friend will grumble at having to get out of bed, but will eventually have to in order to get some peace. In another parable (Luke 18:1-8) he compares prayer to a wronged widow appealing to a judge to take up her case. The judge has no respect for God or concern for people, but in the end he does what she asks because her constant pleas for help are getting him down. Sayings like this reflect the real experience of people who pray, the question "will the answer ever come?" It seems that Jesus might even be saying. "So God doesn't answer your prayers? Pester him till he does!"

The general tenor of the biblical faith is very far from the kind of religion that advocates a calm acceptance of all that is. The clause in the Lord's Prayer that says "thy will be done" is often misunderstood. It is not a prayer of calm acceptance, the belief that whatever happens is God's will. It is a prayer for change, a prayer that God's will may be done here on earth as it is done in the ideal world of Heaven. The Judaeo-Christian kind of spirituality is essentially one of discontent with things as they are and faith that things can be different.

Thanking and Testifying

Often in the psalms a prayer for help and a joyful song of thanksgiving are combined. Psalm 22, for instance, begins "My God, my God, why hast thou forsaken me?", and then suddenly changes mood and becomes a hymn of praise. Many psalms have this pattern: one of the shortest and simplest examples is Psalm 13, which begins with four desperate "how long?" questions, yet ends with: "I will sing to the LORD, because he has dealt bountifully with me".

It seems that often someone in sickness or danger would make a vow, promising to praise God in some special way in the Temple if their prayer was answered. One of the psalms says: "I will come into your house with burnt offerings: I will pay you my vows, those that my lips uttered and my mouth promised when I was in trouble" (Ps 66:13-14). Some psalms tell a story of how someone has prayed and had an answer to their prayer: they are a kind of testimony. One very dramatic example is Psalm 18, which describes the psalmist's plight: "The cords of death encompassed me; the torrents of perdition assailed me". It then goes to say, "In my distress I called upon the LORD", and then "the earth reeled and rocked... He bowed the heavens, and came down... he reached down from on high, he took me; he drew me out of mighty waters".

A psalm of particular interest in this regard is Psalm 107. It begins with an exhortation that is found in several other places: "O give thanks to the LORD, for he is good; for his steadfast love endures forever". It then says: "Let the redeemed of the LORD say so, those he redeemed from trouble", and goes on to graphic descriptions of the different circumstances in which people have prayed and been rescued. Some were lost in the desert, hungry and thirsty; some were in prison; some were sick and dying; some were caught in storms at sea. The psalm closes with a general expression of praise to God and an exhortation to people to be wise and "consider the steadfast love of the LORD". This psalm looks very much like a general liturgy for this kind of prayer, perhaps the opening of a ceremony in which people presented the vows they had made.

Sometimes, however, there is no "happy ending". The prayer is one of pure lament, and apparently unanswered. Psalm 88 is a long litany of complaint by someone who is facing death. Yet, significantly, it begins "O LORD, God of my salvation". It is a prayer to a God who saves, and somehow the psalmist in all his distress and despondency does not lose sight of this. Another psalm that is purely lament is the bitter little prayer of the exiles in Babylon ("By the rivers of Babylon – there we sat down and there we wept") which ends with a wish for vengeance, first on the Edomites who took sides with the Babylonians: "Remember, O LORD, against the Edomites the day of Jerusalem's fall", and then against Babylon itself: "Happy shall they be who take your little ones and dash them against the rock!" (Ps 137)

We can enter into the feelings behind the psalms without necessarily knowing the exact circumstances in which they were first said or sung. Sometimes it is obviously the nation that is in trouble, while at other times the prayer seems very personal. Sometimes we can discern the voice of the king speaking in the first person singular but at the same time on behalf of the nation. Often it is difficult to tell whether a prayer is national or personal. As happens with many hymns, something written in particular circumstances was probably, even within biblical times, found relevant to people in very different situations down through the generations.

The Enemies

One of the most popular passages in the Hebrew scriptures is the twenty-third Psalm ("The LORD is my shepherd") with its atmosphere of quiet confidence in God's protection. It combines two different pictures of God. First there is God the shepherd looking after his sheep, but then the picture changes to that of the generous host welcoming a guest: "Thou anointest mine head with oil; my cup runneth over". However, there is one verse that, for some readers today, may seem to introduce a slightly jarring note: "Thou preparest a table before me in the presence of mine enemies". Why do enemies have to be brought in?

This is in fact a very common feature of the psalms. There seems to be almost an obsession with enemies. We constantly find expressions like "O LORD, how many are my foes! Many are rising against me" (Ps 3:1) and "he delivered me from my strong enemy, and from those who hated me..." (Ps 18:17). In another favourite psalm, one that strikes a chord with us today with its sense of awe in face of the vastness of the universe, we find the saying "Out of the mouths of babes and sucklings hast thou ordained strength because of thine enemies, that thou mightest still the enemy and the avenger" (Ps 8:2). Psalm 104, which praises God for all the gifts of creation and his care for all his creatures, includes just before its final ascription of praise the prayer "let sinners be consumed from the earth, and let the wicked be no more" (Ps 104:35). In fact, of the one hundred and fifty psalms, about a hundred make specific reference to "enemies" or "the wicked", and many of the others feature "victory" and "mighty power" in a way that at least implies the existence of opponents. If the psalms are the songs and prayers of scripture, we cannot escape the impression that the piety of the Hebrew scriptures is one of confrontation.

There are several possible reasons for this constant reference to enemies. First, many of the psalms could have had their origin in early liturgies and rituals designed to boost the soldiers of

Israel as they went to war. They saw the God of Israel as himself leading the battle against his enemies. Psalm 60, for instance, looks like a liturgy before battle. The first few verses are a prayer: "O God, you have rejected us, broken our defences; you have been angry; now restore us!". Then comes an answer: "God has promised in his sanctuary..." This was probably uttered by a priest. It reminds the people how weak and contemptible their enemies are to God (including the memorable phrase "Moab is my washpot"!). Then the prayer is resumed, but the psalm closes with an affirmation of faith: "through God we shall do valiantly: for he it is that shall tread down our enemies".

Secondly, there are psalms that reflect the long periods during which the Jews were an oppressed people, under constant attack. This could apply not only to the community as a whole, but also to individuals in exile, suffering the contempt and mockery of those who scorned their way of life. Many saw their faith as a witness against a world that was universally ungodly, cruel and corrupt. Psalms are full of expressions like "in arrogance the wicked persecute the poor" (Ps 10:2), "help, O LORD, for there is no longer anyone who is godly; the faithful have disappeared from humankind" (Ps 12:1), and "the fool hath said in his heart, there is no God" (Ps 14:1). The psalmists see themselves as suffering for their faithfulness to God, and appeal to God for help against those who mock or persecute them.

Thirdly, there is a type of psalm that seems to belong in the sphere of criminal trials. People accused of a crime would sometimes have to go through some sort of ordeal to establish their innocence, and would pray to God for a favourable outcome. In the process of this prayer they would sometimes denounce and curse the enemies who had brought the accusation against them. Psalm 17 fairly obviously belongs to this category. It begins: "Hear a just cause, O LORD... give ear to my prayer from lips free of deceit". There seems to be a reference to some nocturnal ordeal: "If you try my heart, if you visit me by night, if you test me, you will find no wickedness in me". Then at the end: "when I awake I shall be satisfied, beholding your likeness".

A favourite psalm of many people today is Psalm 139 ("O LORD, you have searched me and known me"). This is often used devotionally because it is such a beautiful expression of intimacy with God. It talks of God's presence in every part of daily life: "You know when I sit down and when I rise up". It talks of the omnipresence of God: "Where can I go from your spirit? Or where can I flee from your presence? If I ascend to heaven, you are there; if I make my bed in Sheol[1], you are there". The psalmist is overwhelmed with the thought of God's intimate knowledge of him from the very beginning of life: "For it was you who formed my inward parts; you knit me together in my mother's womb. I praise you, for I am fearfully and wonderfully made".

But then towards the end there are some verses that are nearly always omitted when the psalm is read in public: "O that you would kill the wicked, O God... Do I not hate those who hate you, O LORD? And do I not loathe those who rise up against you? I hate them with perfect hatred; I count them my enemies". This seems so out of keeping with the warm, trusting, intimate character of the earlier verses that we feel bound to ask what is the connection between these two aspects of the psalm. However, looking more closely at the earlier part, we can see that the emphasis is on God knowing all the secrets of the person praying: nothing is hidden from God's sight. The person is actually asserting his innocence, of which his hatred of God's enemies is added evidence. It is as if he is saying, "God, you know me through and through: you know whose side I'm on". Whatever we think of the sentiments expressed in these few verses, we can see the psalm making sense as a whole if we interpret it as the prayer of someone about to go through an ordeal for judgment. The prayer "Search me, O God, and know my heart; test me and know my thoughts" is probably a very practical plea for a favourable outcome to the ordeal.

To many of us today the psalms seem to have a rather paranoid pre-occupation with enemies. However, this may well be a reflection of the comfortable situation of the majority of church-goers in the Western world who sing these psalms every Sunday or read them in their private devotions. In our relatively peaceful life, protected by an adequate income and an orderly society, we tend to feel we have no real enemies. Our peace of mind is threatened more by sickness, stress, or the fear of old age and death than it is by other people. However, for the so-called "under-class" in the more affluent nations and the majority of the population in the poorer countries, human enemies are an everyday reality. Life for them is often a daily struggle against the unscrupulous employer, the neglectful landlord, the money-lender, the drug-pusher, the neighbourhood gangs and corrupt police, not to mention in some places the ever-present threat of terrorism. It is perhaps in societies like this that many of the psalms, not sanitized or "spiritualized" but simply read as they are, have an immediate relevance. They are a desperate cry for help in a rough world.

Challenging God

The prayers we find in the Bible are not always respectful and submissive. People who are in desperate need can often be demanding, challenging and impertinent, and some of the characters in the Bible could be like that with God. We find them asserting their innocence and questioning the way God is treating them. The psalmists come out with such prayers as: "Why, O LORD, do you stand afar off? Why do you hide yourself in times of trouble?" (Ps 10:1). An interesting example of this reproachful kind of prayer is Psalm 44. It begins by recalling the great deeds God did for "our ancestors", and then goes on to a little song of praise that ends with: "In God we have boasted continually, and we will give thanks to your name forever". But then the mood changes. Perhaps this first part was an old hymn of praise, and the rest of the psalm was added later when circumstances were entirely different. It says, "Yet you have rejected and abased us, and have not gone out with our armies", and goes on to describe repeated defeats, the scattering of the people among the nations, their humiliation and disgrace in the sight of other nations, and so on. There is no sense of deserved suffering here: "All this has come upon us, yet we have not forgotten you, or been false to your covenant". They urge God to wake up: "Rouse yourself! Why do you sleep, O LORD?" Yet their final appeal shows an underlying trusting relationship: "Redeem us for the sake of your steadfast love".

One passage in the Book of Isaiah actually seems to throw onto God the responsibility for the people's sins: "Why, O LORD, do you make us stray from your ways and harden our heart, so that we do not fear you?" (Is 63:17).

Argument with God is a feature of a number of the characters in the Hebrew scriptures. When Moses, after much hesitation and making of excuses, finally obeyed God's call to go to Pharaoh and demand the release of the slaves, the immediate effect was to make the situation worse. Pharaoh instructed the task-masters to tell the slaves they must find their own straw for making bricks and still produce the same daily quota. Then Moses came back to God and said: "O LORD, why have you mistreated this people? Why did you ever send me?... you have done nothing at all to deliver your people" (Ex 5:22-23). Later he complains to God about the burden of coping with this ungrateful, constantly complaining people: "Why have you treated your servant so badly? Why have I not found favour in your sight, that you lay the burden of all this people on me? Did I conceive all this people? Did I give birth to them...? I am not able to carry all this people alone, for they are too heavy for me. If this is the way you are going to treat me, put me to death at once" (Num 11:11-15).

The prophet Jeremiah, too, argues with God. Complaining of his pain and anguish over the plight of his people, he accuses God of letting him down. At first, he says, God's words were a joy and delight to him, but now he asks why his pain is unceasing: "Truly, you are to me like a deceitful brook, like waters that fail" (Jer 15:16-18).

This questioning, arguing relationship reaches its greatest dramatic intensity in the Book of Job. There we find a man who is suffering. Though he has lived a blameless and upright life, he has lost his family, his fortune and his health, and wants to know why. In one of the most obvious examples of the Bible "arguing with itself", he takes up the awe-struck question of the psalmist "what are human beings, that you are mindful of them, mortals that you care for them?" (Ps 8:4) and turns it into a bitter reproach: "What are human beings, that you make so much of them, that you set your mind on them, visit them every morning, test them every moment?" (Job 7:17-18). He wants to say to God: "Does it seem good to you to oppress, to despise the work of your hands...?" (Job 10:3). He longs to be able to find out where God is so that he can confront him face to face: "I would lay my case before him, and fill my mouth with arguments. I would learn what he would answer me, and understand what he would say to me" (Job 23:4-5). Though he recognizes the infinite superiority of God, there is no grovelling in his attitude. He is aware of his right to dignity even in the presence of God: "like a prince I would approach him" (Job 31:37). All this questioning raises the fundamental issue of the justice of God, an issue to which we shall return in chapter 7.

There is something of this in the Jewish faith to this day. There are many stories in Jewish tradition that question some of the stories and teachings of the Bible, or talk of conversations in which a believer bargains with God or engages in humorous, ironic banter with him. It can also be deadly serious, as in the story of a group of prisoners in Auschwitz who decided to put

God on trial. They found that God, if not actually guilty, at least had a real case to answer, and then the trial was adjourned because it was time to say their prayers!

Christians have tended to play down this aspect of the relationship between God and the believer, laying more stress on surrender and acceptance. There are hints that Jesus had more of that kind of relationship with God than his later followers realised or were able to accept. In the garden of Gethsemane we find him pleading with God to take away the cup of suffering before he finally surrenders to what God wants (Matt 26:39; Mark 14:36; Luke 22:42). On the cross, according to Matthew and Mark, he quoted Psalm 22 and cried: "My God, my God, why have you forsaken me?" (Matt 27:46; Mark 15:34).

The comparative lack of this questioning, challenging element in much Christian piety probably stems from the influence of Greek philosophy in the shaping of Christianity. While Jews have a sense of a God who is a real personality and is related to them in a special way, Christians tend to think of God in a more universal and theoretical way. They therefore feel the need to acknowledge that because God is universal love everything God does is somehow for the best. This encourages a piety that stresses acceptance and surrender rather than questioning. The kind of relationship with God that we find in the Jewish scriptures perhaps needs to be taken more seriously by Christians if we are to have an authentic spirituality that connects to our real experience today. Questioning and arguing are often part of the necessary journey to deeper faith and the sense of a closer relationship with God. In the Book of Psalms, Job, Jeremiah and many other places we can watch the struggle of a desperate person through doubt to faith. This is no serene, unshaken trust in all things being well. It is the acknowledgment that the cry for help is not always heard, and the quest for some kind of answer to the question "why?"

We tend today to ask the question in a philosophical way, but the people who produced the Bible, with their vivid sense of a personal God, argued directly with God. The logic of biblical prayer is that God is open to persuasion: if this were not the case, there would be no point in praying. Sometimes in the Bible we even find references to God changing his mind. He changed his mind when Moses pleaded with him not to destroy the people after they had made the golden calf (Ex 32:14). He changed his mind about destroying the city of Nineveh when the people repented in response to Jonah's preaching (Jon 3:10). God is said to turn from his anger and withdraw his wrath (Ps 85:3). Hosea even talks of God being inwardly torn and unable to make up his mind (Hos 11:8). This concept is difficult to reconcile with our classical perception of God, influenced as it is by Greek philosophy, but in the light of the uncertainty principle that is being discovered by scientists in our time it may be worth reconsidering. Perhaps after all the universe is not a closed system but an open, dynamic process in which human aspirations and prayers can actually make a difference.

However that may be, the faith of many of the writers of the Bible was as vulnerable and as open to doubt as the faith of any of us today. It was not a calm certainty, but a passionate, even desperate attempt to hold on to a powerful and merciful God when all the evidence seemed to be stacked against such a God being there. We today may interpret things in a more intellectual way and ask different questions, but biblical prayers can still touch a nerve in our real experience.

Notes

1. See Note 1 to Chapter 4.

7

Crying for Justice

"Shall not the Judge of all the earth do right?"
(Gen 18:25)

Anyone who has tried to read the Bible from beginning to end expecting a good story will have discovered that a very large part of the books of Exodus, Leviticus, Numbers and Deuteronomy is taken up with laws. Some of them are instructions for ritual, feasts, the design of the Temple and so on, but many of them are about the details of everyday life in the community. They concern the appropriate penalty for violent behaviour, procedures to follow when farm animals cause damage, injury or death, and various other issues to do with property. In these laws we can see the attempt of a community to work out just and fair ways of living together. Some of them may be no longer relevant to us, and some now seem unfair and harsh. We cannot read them today as direct divine prescriptions for our society. The culture that produced them was very different from ours, with taboos that often mean nothing to us. Yet across the culture gap we can still recognize the determined ongoing effort to work out what is fair and just.

The Prophets' Passion

This concern was not just a cool legalistic one. The prophets, alongside their concern for the pure and exclusive worship of the one God, were equally as concerned about social justice. One of the earliest examples of a prophet standing for justice is Nathan's confronting of King David (2 Sam 11-12). David, who already had several wives, had an affair with Bathsheba, the wife of Uriah, who was away on the battlefield. When Bathsheba became pregnant, David called Uriah home and tried to get him to sleep with her so that he would think the child was his own. Uriah, however, had too stern a sense of his duty as a soldier to do this, so the trick didn't work. David then sent Uriah back with a confidential letter to the commander of his army instructing him to station Uriah in a dangerous place and leave him unprotected. This plan worked, and Uriah was killed, leaving David free to marry Bathsheba. However, the prophet Nathan knew what he had done and confronted him with it. The interesting thing about this is that Nathan did not quote the commandment against adultery. He told David a story about a man who had a huge flock of sheep and robbed his poor neighbour of the one pet lamb he had. When David declared that the man who did that deserved to die, Nathan simply said "You are the man!" Nathan presented the situation not as the breaking of a sexual taboo but as a simple matter of justice.

Those who wrote the history of Israel took great pride in the wealth and splendour of the kingdom of David and Solomon, but at the same time there is a strong element of criticism and frequent reminders that a king is judged by how justly he rules, and especially by how he treats the poorest of his subjects. This principle is clear in Psalm 72. The opening of the psalm, with its reference to "the king" and "a king's son", seems to indicate that it was a coronation hymn. Much of it echoes the traditional "hype" that was loaded onto the rulers of the time: "May he have dominion from sea to sea, and from the River to the ends of the earth. May his foes bow down before him, and his enemies lick the dust. May the kings of Tarshish and the isles render him tribute", and so on. But there is embedded within it a strong element of concern for justice. It begins with: "Give the king your justice, O God, and your righteousness to a king's son. May he judge your people with righteousness, and your poor with justice... May he defend the cause of the poor of the people, give deliverance to the needy, and crush the oppressor". Then, after the wishes for power and prosperity, the psalm returns to the same theme: "For he delivers the needy when they call, the poor and those who have no helper".

The "writing" prophets (those whose names are given to biblical books) preached very passionately against injustice. Their books contain some of the most damning descriptions of the contrast between the rich and the poor and the fiercest condemnation of the greed and corruption that created this inequality. Isaiah asserts that the point has been reached where God hates the worship the people offer to him: "even though you make many prayers, I will not listen; your hands are full of blood... cease to do evil, learn to do good; seek justice, rescue the oppressed, defend the orphan, plead for the widow" (Is 1:12-17). He attacks the greedy land owners who "join house to house, who add field to field, until there is room for no one but you" (Is 5:8).

The prophet Amos denounces those who "sell the righteous for silver, and the needy for a pair of sandals... who trample the head of the poor into the dust of the earth" (Amos 2:6-7). He attacks the rich women of Samaria, calling them "cows of Bashan" (Amos 4:1). Bashan was a rich, fertile area noted for its fat cattle. We do not know whether calling a woman a "cow" had quite the same connotations then that it has in English today, but it certainly could not have been complimentary! He satirizes those who, while piously celebrating a holy festival, are impatient for it to be over so that they can get back to their normal business of profiteering, cheating and exploiting the poor (Amos 8:4-6).

Micah attacks those who "tear the skin off my people, and the flesh off their bones" (Mic 3:2), the rulers who take bribes and the priests and prophets who are only in it for the money (Mic 3:11). He asserts the pointlessness of extreme ritual sacrifices and says: "what does the LORD require of you but to do justice, and to love kindness, and to walk humbly with your God?" (Mic 6:6-8).

When reading the prophets we can often feel the passion that motivated them. We may not always understand what the issue was, because there are frequent references to people or to events we know little or nothing about, but we can identify with the anger they felt about the inequality of society. We must of course beware of thinking of them as "left wing" or "socialists": this would be an anachronism. They had not developed theories about labour and capital, but they spoke from a strong sense of Israel being a family and its land being God's gift. To them it was not right that within the family some should be amassing wealth while others went hungry. Nor was it right that the family's heritage of land should be taken into the hands of greedy individuals or handed over to strangers.

At the same time there was a more general sense of human justice. This comes out in the way that the prophets sometimes call other nations to account for their acts of oppression and cruelty (as in Amos 1:3 – 2:3).

Jesus shared the prophets' passionate concern for justice. He denounced the teachers of the law who took advantage of the simple piety of poor people or practised exploitation in their business dealings: "They devour widows' houses and for the sake of appearance say long prayers" (Mark 12:40). He pleaded for a breaking down of class discrimination, exhorting people when they hold a banquet not to confine their invitations to their own kind who will return the invitation, but to invite "the poor, the crippled, the lame and the blind" (Luke 14:12-14).

Among the New Testament writers outside the Gospels, it is James who holds most closely to this theme. He challenges the Christian congregations who pay flattering attention to rich visitors while humiliating the poor (Jas 2:1-6), and fires a diatribe against rich people who exploit their workers. In language that strongly echoes that of the prophets, he says: "The wages of the labourers who mowed your fields, which you kept back by fraud, cry out, and the cries of the harvesters have reached the ears of the Lord of hosts" (Jas 5:4).

The Bible writers were in no doubt that injustice, just as much as idolatry, came under the judgment of God, and punishment would come sooner or later. Jesus referred to "the day of judgment" (Matt 10:15; 11:22.24 etc.), and delineated it vividly in the parable of the sheep and the goats (Matt 25:31-46). Paul talks of the wrath of God being revealed against all ungodliness and wickedness, and goes on to say how everyone will be repaid according to their deeds (Rom 1:18; 2:5-10). Both Daniel and Revelation describe the final judgment as the opening of books in which all the deeds of human beings are recorded (Dan 7:10; Rev 20:12). The Hebrew scriptures generally concentrate more on people's deeds being rewarded during their earthly life or the life of their descendants. As we have seen, the whole history of Israel from Judges to 2 Kings, under the influence of the prophets, was written with this interpretation.

This idea of divine judgment, reward and punishment is not one that appeals to most of us today. Many people prefer to think in terms of karma, the Eastern belief that there is an inevitable universal process by which "what goes round comes round". Something of this is seen even in the Bible, with observations like "you reap whatever you sow" (Gal 6:7). Even Christian preachers today prefer not to talk about God rewarding and punishing, but rather to point to the natural consequences of selfishness, greed and deceit.

However, one thing that can be said for the biblical viewpoint is that it is a way out of the inevitability of karma. The concept of karma may make the universal reality or Spirit seem kinder than the wrathful biblical God, but it is worth asking whether it really is such good news. Is there any escape from karma, or are we destined throughout this life and future lives to live with the karma we have created? We cannot argue with an impersonal natural process, but the Bible talks of a God who judges but can also forgive. To forgive is to wipe away what has been wrong, to heal the wounds, to break the chain of consequences. Biblical faith imagines a God who is able to turn the bad into good. At the end of the story of Joseph we find him saying to his brothers, "Even though you intended to do harm to me, God intended it for good..." (Gen 50:20). In the New Testament story the worst sin imaginable, the crucifixion of the Son of God, did not create a great wave of bad karma, but was turned into salvation for the world. Admittedly, Christian bigotry and racism down through the centuries have made it bad karma for the Jews, but thankfully we are now at last beginning to see that tragic misunderstanding for what it was.

Turning the Tables

The Bible is full of stories about God taking sides with those who are the lowest in the world's estimation. It is thought that the biblical idea of monotheism owes something to the Egyptian background: the Egyptians too believed in one God. However, while for the Egyptians the one God was represented on earth by the one king to whom all the lower classes were subservient, in the biblical story the one God was with the Hebrew slaves who were the bottom layer of Egyptian society, and "heard their cry".

The stories in the Hebrew scriptures often tell of the weak overcoming the strong. Perhaps the story of David and Goliath is the most popular. There is also the story of how Gideon deliberately reduced his army from 32,000 to 300 and defeated the powerful Midianites with the help of God (Judg 7:2-7).

When the fortunes of Israel declined, the people were scattered in exile, and the land was almost permanently occupied by foreign empires, the Jews held onto their faith that God was still on their side. This often expressed itself in dreams of the kingdom being restored and becoming free and prosperous again. The Book of Isaiah talks of the Jews being rewarded with superior status as a double compensation for all the oppression they had suffered: "Strangers shall stand and feed your flocks, foreigners shall till your land and dress your vines" (Is 61:5-7).

However, there also grew the insight that somehow their very poverty and humiliation made them in some way special. This reaches its supreme expression in the fifty-third chapter of Isaiah with the portrait of one who is "despised and rejected of men, a man of sorrows and acquainted with grief", cut off from the land of the living, and yet counted by God as one of the great and the strong. Christians from the very beginning saw this portrait of the Suffering Servant as a portrait of Christ.

In the story of the birth of Samuel to Hannah, who had long been thought incapable of having children, we find her song (1 Sam 2:1-10) in which she praises the God who reverses fortunes: "Those who were full have hired themselves out for bread, but those who were hungry are fat with spoil. The barren has borne seven, but she who has many children is forlorn". The song of Mary in the New Testament, the "Magnificat" (Luke 2:46-55), is largely based on Hannah's song, saying things like "He hath put down the mighty from their seats, and exalted them of low degree. He hath filled the hungry with good things, and the rich he hath sent empty away".

This sense of the turning of the tables is prominent too in the teaching of Jesus, in revolutionary sayings like "Blessed are you who are poor, for yours is the kingdom of God. Blessed are you who are hungry now, for you will be filled. Blessed are you who weep now, for you will laugh... But woe to you who are rich, for you have received your consolation. Woe to you who are full now, for you will be hungry. Woe to you who are laughing now, for you will mourn and weep" (Luke 6:20-26).

This biblical bias towards the poor and despised is still today a rich vein of inspiration for Christians expressing their concern for the rights of minorities and marginalized people. Many approaches to theology today, with labels like "liberation", "black", "post-colonial", "feminist", "gay" and so on are all engaged in this ongoing quest to implement God's bias to the poor, the despised and the marginalized. They challenge the way in which established authorities have used the more hierarchical, patriarchal parts of the Bible to justify their own power, and they turn instead to the much more basic biblical emphasis on the "underdog".

This "upside down" world dreamed of by the Bible writers expresses itself not only in a bias towards the poor and oppressed, but in other ways too. There is for instance the repeated motif of the youngest brother. Jacob and Esau were twins, but though Esau was the first-born it was Jacob who was blessed by God and became father of the people (Gen 25:19-34 etc.). It was Joseph, the youngest but one of Jacob's sons, and the most despised and ill-treated, who rose to power in Egypt and was able to save the whole family from starvation (Gen 37; 39ff). When God sent Samuel to the home of Jesse in Bethlehem to anoint the future king of Israel, the one chosen was David, the youngest son who had not even been presented to Samuel but left out in the field to look after the sheep (1 Sam 16:1-13).

Paul expounds this theme in relation to the nature of the Christian community. He points out to the church in Corinth that very few of them are highly educated, powerful or of noble birth, and with his great gift for paradox goes on to say: "But God chose what is foolish in the world to shame the wise... what is weak in the world to shame the strong... what is low and despised in the world, things that are not, to reduce to nothing things that are" (1 Cor 1:27-28)

Does God Act Justly?

The Hebrew scriptures are very much taken up with the belief that God rewards the good with long life and prosperity, and punishes those who disobey him. Not only in the history of the nation but also in the life of the individual, this principle was believed to be universal. It is expressed in such places as the first Psalm: "Blessed is the man that walketh not in the counsel of the ungodly... whatsoever he doeth shall prosper. The ungodly are not so: but are like the chaff, which the wind driveth away."

Psalm 37 ("Fret not thyself because of evildoers") is a long discourse asserting that, though ungodly and unrighteous people may seem to prosper for a time, in the long run God's justice never fails. The writer exhorts the reader to "rest in the LORD, and wait patiently for him" (v7), and testifies: "I have been young, and am now old, yet I have not seen the righteous forsaken or their children begging bread" (v25). However, the very fact that such a psalm needed to be written shows that this principle of reward and punishment was not always easy to believe. There are in fact many parts of the Bible where it is questioned, and where people challenge God as to whether he is doing right.

One of the earliest is the story of Abraham bargaining with God about his plan to destroy the city of Sodom (Gen 18:17-33). God reveals to Abraham that he is planning to destroy the city because of its wickedness, but Abraham is concerned about the righteous people who may be living there, one of whom is his own nephew Lot. God assures Abraham that if he can find fifty righteous men he will spare the whole city. However, Abraham then wonders what will happen if there are less than fifty. He is aware that he is perhaps over-stepping the mark in presuming to argue with God in this way: "Let me take it upon myself to speak to the Lord, I who am but dust and ashes" (v27). Nevertheless he perseveres, and step by step brings the number down from fifty to ten. At that point the dialogue ends, and we are left wondering what would have happened if Abraham had taken it even further. This too is part of the Bible's character. Sometimes the writers speak as eloquently with their silences as with their words. What is not said invites the reader to take up the quest for understanding and pursue it further. This story has a suggestion of the oriental market-place about it, but this is no selfish haggling. It is an exploration of what the justice of God really means. The key question is: "shall not the Judge of all the earth do right?" (Gen 18:25, AV) The faith of those who wrote the Hebrew scriptures was not a passive, unquestioning submission to God. It was a passionate, often provocative quest for a truly just God, an appeal to God's sense of fair play.

This question of the justice of God reaches its greatest and most passionate expression in the Book of Job. Job is an upright man of exemplary piety, but one day he loses all his property and all his sons and their families are killed. He responds to all this with calm acceptance: "The LORD gave, and the LORD has taken away; blessed be the name of the LORD". Even when he loses his health too, and is afflicted with loathsome sores from head to foot, his initial reaction is: "Shall we receive the good at the hand of God, and not receive the bad?" This is all in the prose introduction to the book, but in the poetic bulk of it the tone is different. Some of Job's friends come to "comfort" him, repeating all the platitudes of faith. They assume that he is being punished for some sin, and urge him to repent and turn to God. But Job refuses to accept this interpretation of his suffering. He is determined to resist their easy, pious answers and to argue directly with God. He accuses his friends of trying to defend God with weak arguments: "As for you, you whitewash with lies... Will you speak falsely for God, and speak deceitfully for him?... Your maxims are proverbs of ashes, your defences are defences of clay" (Job 13:4-12).

Then, in the midst of his despair, he comes out with a statement that has intrigued scholars and preachers down through the ages: "For I know that my Redeemer lives, and that at last he will stand upon the earth, and after my skin has been thus destroyed, then in my flesh I shall see God, whom I shall see on my side" (Job 19:25-27). This is a very difficult passage to interpret (see our discussion in Chapter 9), but there is certainly within it an expression of Job's confidence that in the end God will prove to be on his side.

The character called Job is legendary, and has no place in any of the genealogies or histories of Israel. He is a generic human being, invented in order to raise the question: "Suppose a man of perfect character, faith and piety were to suffer the greatest extremity of misfortune, would this disprove the justice of God?" The book does not end with an answer: how could it? The only conclusion seems to be that God is the Creator of the world and does not have to justify himself to Job or anyone else. And yet in the end God commends the rebellious, questioning Job rather than his pious and thoroughly orthodox friends. The implication seems to be that even though there is no answer it is still better to ask the questions than to submit passively to established belief and carry on repeating platitudes that are not convincing.

And so, even though parts of the Bible speak of the justice of God as if it were transparent and simple, there were those among the Bible writers who recognized that in the reality of this world God's justice, like everything else about God, is elusive.

8

Looking for Love

It is generally assumed today that Christianity is meant to be a religion of love. Almost certainly the most frequently quoted saying of Jesus is "love your neighbour as yourself", (Matt 22:34-40 etc., quoted from Lev 19:18). The whole Christian message is often summed up in quotations like "God so loved the world that he gave his only Son" (John 3:16), and the simple, absolute statement that "God is love" (1 John 4:8.16). The Christian church at its best is seen as a mission that provides people with pastoral support in all the different circumstances of life and reaches out indiscriminately to help those in need. In places where Christians are engaged in war against one another, or where they espouse aggressive political views and extremely judgmental attitudes, the general reaction of most people is to express incredulity that Christians can be so unloving. Though "see how these Christians love one another" is more often heard today as a bitter irony, the general perception is that it ought to be a positive truth. The greatest reproach to which the church is open is that it does not live up to its essential message of love.

This reproach could in many ways be directed to the Bible too. Taking the Bible as a whole, it is not obvious that love is its main theme. The God of the Hebrew scriptures usually comes over as one whose chief quality is power, and sometimes a power that is used in an arbitrary way. The concept of the justice of God, as we have seen, is often expressed in terms of punishment that is sometimes very harsh. Very early in the Bible we have the story of God destroying the human race with a flood because he was angry with them. Later we read how he rescued his chosen people from slavery in Egypt by inflicting ten terrible plagues on the Egyptians and drowning their entire army in the sea. Even the chosen people were not immune from extreme punishment. On the way to the Promised Land, as a punishment for rebelling against Moses' leadership, God made the earth open and swallow up two hundred and fifty of them, and then inflicted a plague on the people that killed fourteen thousand seven hundred more (Num 16:49). In the New Testament too there often seems to be a preoccupation with sin, judgment and arguments about doctrine rather than love. As in the church, so in the Bible, belief in a God of love seems to have to battle its way through a huge load of reality that contradicts it.

On the other hand there is no doubt that, amid all the primitive fears and superstitions, the legalism and the militarism, the Bible documents an earnest quest for a loving God.

At a relatively simple level, we can see how the system of justice developed among the Israelites always included a strong element of compassion. A simple law that is worth thinking about in this age of ruthless profit-making and cost-cutting is found in the Book of Leviticus: "When you reap the harvest of your land, you shall not reap to the very edges of your field, or gather the gleanings of your harvest. You shall not strip your vineyard bare, or gather the fallen grapes of your vineyard; you shall leave them for the poor and the alien" (Lev 19:9-10; cf. Deut 24:19-22). One of the laws says that if a poor man borrows money and gives the creditor his cloak as security, the cloak must be returned to him at night so that he can sleep in it (Deut 24:12-13).

The commandment "love your neighbour as yourself" first appears in a block of legal material (Lev 19:18). The same chapter actually commands the Israelites to respect the aliens who live among them, remembering that they themselves were once aliens in Egypt. It goes so far as to say, "you shall love the alien as yourself" (Lev 19:34). In the directions for the harvest festival the people are reminded that "the Levites and the aliens" should join in the celebrations (Deut 26:11). The Levites were the priestly tribe who had no land and so no harvest of their own to celebrate, but who served the people in their special way. However, it is noteworthy that the landless aliens are included too. The tithe of the produce of the land was to be given to "the Levites, the aliens, the orphans, and the widows" (Deut 26:12).

There was also the law of the Jubilee (Lev 25). Every fiftieth year was specially sanctified. In it, debts were to be cancelled, all land was to be returned to the family to which it had originally belonged, and all bonded labourers were to be released. It is difficult to imagine how often this law was observed, if at all, and certainly once the land was taken over by the surrounding empires there was little or no chance of implementing it. However, its very existence as an aspiration is testimony to a deep sense of social solidarity in the nation of Israel that went beyond mere legal contracts and rights.

God's Love for His Chosen

In the Hebrew scriptures the language of love as such is most frequently found in the portrayal of God's love for Israel as his chosen people. There is an element of arbitrary choice in this. God, in his sovereignty, favours whom he pleases: "I will be gracious to whom I will be gracious, and will show mercy on whom I will show mercy" (Ex 33:19). There is often more talk of God's "favour" than of his love. It seems that the people behind the Hebrew scriptures experienced their God as one who could destroy them or bless them according to whether they had "found favour" in his sight. This favour was often quite unpredictable. One of the first stories in the Bible tells how God accepted the sacrifice Abel offered but rejected Cain's, and no reason is given (Gen 4:4-5). Later we find that God's promise to create a great and privileged nation is fulfilled through Jacob, the younger of twins, again for no apparent reason. The arbitrary nature of this choice is bluntly put: "I have loved Jacob, but I have hated Esau" (Mal 1:2-3; compare Rom 9:13).

Deuteronomy has God saying to the Israelites:

"It was not because you were more numerous than any other people that the LORD set his heart on you and chose you – for you were the fewest of all peoples. It was because the LORD loved you and kept the oath that he swore to your ancestors, that the LORD has brought you out with a mighty hand, and redeemed you from the house of slavery" (Deut 7:7-8).

This love has a strong element of jealousy. The commandment to worship no other god is followed by the statement: "I the LORD your God am a jealous God" (Ex 20:5).

In many parts of the Hebrew scriptures, it is not so much the tender two-way caring relationship we usually think of as love that is featured, but the dominating, possessive relationship of men to their women in a thoroughly patriarchal society. Israel is often represented as God's wife, which means in effect that she is his property and that she owes him absolute fidelity and obedience. The worship of other gods is often labelled as adultery. It could even be compared with a wife who leaves her husband and turns to prostitution. Jeremiah, probably thinking of the hilltop shrines to other gods, says to the people, "long ago you broke your yoke and burst your bonds, and you said, 'I will not serve!' On every high hill and under every green tree you sprawled and played the whore" (Jer 2:20). "Look up to the bare heights and see! Where have you not been lain with?" (Jer 3:2).

Ezekiel paints a lurid picture in which God tells the nation of Judah how he found her as an abandoned child, cast out and bleeding, and how he took her in, cleaned her up, and cared for her till she became a grown woman, how he dressed her in finery and showered her with gifts, and how she then became a whore offering herself to every passer-by and bringing utter disgrace upon herself. Judah, he says (Ezek 16), is worse than a whore: a whore at least gets paid for her services, but Judah, in offering gifts to all the other gods, is more like a woman so lustful that she *pays* men to come to her!

Much of this patriarchal imagery is distasteful and morally repugnant to us today. There is something raw, passionate and strongly sexual about the God of the Hebrew prophets. Far from thinking of God as high above all fleshly passions, they had no hesitation in projecting onto God the feelings of sexual desire and jealousy that were part of their life, expressed and legitimated within the norms of their culture.

At the same time, there are places where (as happens in the most patriarchal of societies) a more tender expression of love breaks through. The prophet Hosea seems to have enacted in his own life the ways of God with his unfaithful people. He says that God told him to marry a whore, and describes how the ups and downs of their relationship reflect the ups and downs of God's relationship with Israel. Like Hosea himself, wanting to expose and punish his wife and yet still taking her back because he cannot stop loving her, God is torn between rage and tenderness. God threatens all kinds of punishment to his people for their unfaithfulness, but then turns and says things like "I will now persuade her, and bring her into the wilderness, and speak tenderly to her... There she shall respond as in the days of her youth, at the time when she came out of the land of Egypt" (Hos 2:14-15).

Later the metaphor changes to the beautiful, tender picture of a parent with a little child: "it was I who taught Ephraim to walk, I took them up in my arms... I led them with cords of human kindness, with bands of love. I was to them like those who lift infants to their cheeks. I bent down to them and fed them". Then after another outburst of anger comes a picture of God torn between anger and love: "How can I give you up, Ephraim? How can I hand you over, O Israel?... My heart recoils within me; my compassion grows warm and tender. I will not execute my fierce anger" (Hos 11:1-9).

Later we find the prophet of restoration after the Exile saying "Comfort, O comfort my people, says your God. Speak tenderly to Jerusalem...", and the image of a shepherd bringing the sheep home, gathering the lambs in his arms and gently leading the mother sheep (Is 40:1-2.11). Clearly some at least of the prophets had a warm, tender conception of the love of God for Israel.

There are other passages too where the love and forgiveness of God are more strongly emphasized than his punitive justice. Psalm 103 includes a warm affirmation of God's loving and forgiving nature: "The LORD is merciful and gracious, slow to anger and abounding in steadfast love". It goes on to talk of how God forgives the sins of human beings because "he remembers that we are dust". Even here, however, the fatherly compassion of God is directed to "those who fear him" (Ps 103:8-14). Another psalm goes further, and says: "The LORD is good to all, and his compassion is over all that he has made" (Ps 145:9).

It seems, then, that the writers of the Hebrew scriptures did not come easily to the concept of a God of universal love. Most of them were either interpreting their own experience of a rough world in which the "favour" of God was unpredictable, or else projecting onto God their own need to punish their enemies. Just here and there we find them reaching out in hope and faith to find a God of love, first for themselves and ultimately for the whole world.

Looking for Mercy

A strong theme throughout the Bible, and one that continues into most traditions of Christianity, is the quest for a merciful, forgiving God. Psalm 51 ("Have mercy upon me, O God, according to thy loving kindness") is one of the most moving expressions of the experience of guilt, coming from "a broken and a contrite heart" (Ps 51:17).

Guilt is not always personal. In the Jewish scriptures there is a strong element of national guilt. The prophets were constantly reminding the Israelites that they were meant to be the people of God, bound in a covenant to worship the one God and obey his commandments. That covenant, it seemed to them, was constantly being broken, and the defeats and disasters that came upon the nation were God's judgment. After the Exile, when Jerusalem had been destroyed by the Babylonians and the people taken away from the land, this sense of national guilt became the leading theme in the interpretation of Israel's history.

At the same time, there was a conviction that the God who judged could also forgive, and having destroyed he could also restore. About fifty years after the Babylonian conquest destroyed Jerusalem and took many of its citizens into exile, Babylon itself was taken over by the Persian king Cyrus, who encouraged Jews to return to their land and rebuild Jerusalem. The anonymous prophet behind the second part of Isaiah exulted in this as a sign that God was turning again and restoring the people to his favour. The way in which the message is worded seems even to suggest that God has overdone the judgment a bit and now wants to make up for it. The "tender" message to Jerusalem was that "she has served her term, that her penalty is paid, that she has received from the LORD's hand double for all her sins" (Is 40:2).

After this exciting promise, things did not go as smoothly as was hoped. Some of the Jews returned to their country, Jerusalem was restored to some extent and the Temple rebuilt, but things were not quite the same as they had been before the Exile, and there were long periods of struggle and disappointment. A heavy sense of guilt still hung over many of the people. We see it expressed in the prayer of Ezra: "O my God, I am too ashamed and embarrassed to lift my face to you, my God, for our iniquities have risen higher than our heads, and our guilt has mounted up to the heavens. From the days of our ancestors to this day we have been deep in guilt..." (Ezra 9:6-7)

This sense of being under judgment was reinforced by the

experience of the following centuries, as the Jewish community lived through the rule of the Persians, the conquests of Alexander, the often brutally oppressive rule of his Syrian successors, the brief and fragile independence under the successors of the Maccabees, and then absorption into the Roman Empire. At the same time, there was the increasing anticipation of a better time ahead, of the coming of the Messiah and what was called "the day of the Lord" or "the year of the Lord's favour", a time when God would finally forgive the sins of Israel, restore them fully to his favour, set them free and make them prosperous.

It is against this background that we can see much of the point of the story of Jesus. Luke tells the story of how Jesus, in the synagogue in his home town of Nazareth, read from the Book of Isaiah the passage about preaching the good news to the poor and oppressed and proclaiming "the year of the Lord's favour" (Luke 4:18-19; Is 61:1-2), and then asserted that it was being fulfilled at that moment. In the Gospels we see how Jesus was constantly bringing good news of God's mercy to those in need of it: the "lepers" outcast because of their ritual uncleanness, the "sinners" condemned by the religious leaders, and Gentiles like a Roman army officer or a Canaanite woman. Luke, in particular, sees this proclaiming of forgiveness as the chief point of the ministry of Jesus and of the ongoing preaching of the gospel by his followers.

The theme of forgiveness is taken up, albeit in different and more complicated terms, in the theology Paul expounds in his letters, especially the Letter to the Romans. A particular interpretation of Paul, mainly by Augustine, has left its mark on Western Christianity. Both Roman Catholics and Protestants, in their different ways, have tended to present Christianity mainly in terms of a way of winning forgiveness of sins from a righteous, holy and punishing God. In the Catholic tradition it has been chiefly a matter of sacramental confession, penance and absolution, always with the fear of Hell in the background. The Protestant Reformers rejected all this and preached "justification by faith", the belief that our sins are cancelled once and for all by the death of Jesus on the cross. However, this was basically just a different way of playing the same game. The fear of Hell was as real as ever, and assurance of salvation could only be gained by repentance, and by faith in the sacrifice of Jesus who bore the punishment for our sins on the cross. Protestant preaching and hymns often major on being "washed in the blood", and a sense of the total depravity of human beings and the miracle that God can forgive them. The eighteenth century hymn "Amazing grace, how sweet the sound, that saved a wretch like me!" is still popular, though probably more for its tune than for its words.

For many people today this is the most unacceptable part of biblical spirituality. The ideas that emanate from the "new age" movement are completely different. They tell us that we are divine beings, each one of us beautiful and precious, and that it is only our fear and our low self-esteem that hold us back from realising and expressing our divine nature. The idea that we are sinners needing to repent and be forgiven is probably the greatest stumbling-block present-day spiritual seekers find in Christianity. The biblical emphasis on guilt, atoning sacrifice, and the need for a "merciful" God is quite alien to the spirituality of many people today even within the Christian churches.

The present-day spirituality that encourages people to think of themselves as beautiful and magnificent is largely a reaction to the negative self-image people have grown up with as a result of over-strict parenting, or a particularly narrow, legalistic kind of religion. It also appeals to people who have had their confidence crushed by the pressures of the competitive society we live in. The message people want to hold onto is: whoever you are, whatever label society puts on you, whatever your race, gender or sexuality, whatever your achievements or failures in the world, no matter how much people have made you feel bad about yourself, you are a beautiful, precious person and you are totally accepted for who you are. In Christian terms this is expressed by a slogan popular in many quarters: "Smile, Jesus loves you!"

This may be different from much of the teaching that has characterized both Catholic and Protestant Christianity for centuries, but it may not be so different from the attitude of many of the writers of the Bible. The Hebrew scriptures show little of the idea that human beings are predominantly bad: indeed, they include many stories of God specially favouring those who are despised by others. The message of most of the New Testament is that we are all precious and loved in the sight of God, and we are freely "justified" by God's grace rather than by anything we have achieved. We can see in Jesus a sense of joy and freedom in the presence of a loving God, and a generous acceptance of all kinds of people. Jesus could be scathing about the oppressors and the hypocrites of his time, but he never seems to have gone around preaching to ordinary people about their sin. The religious leaders were scandalized by the way he mingled with people regardless of their purity or piety, and was frequently seen at parties: they even branded him "a glutton and a drunkard" (Matt 11:19). Jesus declared in his teaching and his actions that God's mercy is not something we have to beg for in penitence, but is free and unconditional.

Is God Soft?

This universal and unconditional love of God is sometimes a controversial issue in the Bible. It comes out very sharply in the remarkable little Book of Jonah. This short story is a kind of parable, full of humour and also of deep paradox, meant to make the reader think. God tells the prophet Jonah to go and preach to the people of Nineveh, the capital of the Assyrian empire. He shies off from this call and boards a ship that will take him in another direction altogether. The ship runs into a storm and is in danger of sinking. The sailors (all heathen from the Jewish point of view) pray to their gods. Meanwhile Jonah is asleep. The sailors wake him and demand to know who he is. He utters the proud boast of the Jew: "I am a Hebrew... I worship the LORD, the God of heaven, who made the sea and the dry land" (Jon 1:9). But his boast is invalidated as he makes it by his admission that he has taken to the sea to run away from that God! They try hard to bring the ship to land, but in the end they agree to Jonah's request to throw him into the sea so that the ship will be saved. Then, while Jonah is drowning in the sea, the heathen sailors are offering sacrifices and vows to the God of Israel! Jonah, however, is prevented from drowning by a great fish that swallows him and three days later vomits him out onto dry land.

God then tells Jonah a second time to go to Nineveh and warn the people that their city will be destroyed in forty days. This time he obeys and, much to his surprise, the people of Nineveh from the king down take heed of the message and repent and pray for forgiveness. God then decides to call off the punishment. Jonah takes his seat on a nearby hill to watch the destruction of the city, but nothing happens, and Jonah is not pleased. Then God gently points out to him that the people of Nineveh are human beings too, and asks whether God should not care for all of them, and even for their cattle.

The story is obviously not historical. Like Job, it is a "what if?" story, setting an unlikely scenario to stimulate thought. At first sight it seems to be a satire on the ridiculous moral posturing of the self-righteous, but it is probably much more serious than that. Jonah was not just sulking, he was suicidal. We have to remember that Nineveh was the capital of an empire that had oppressed Israel for centuries. Its people had destroyed the kingdom of Israel altogether, and come very close to destroying Judah. The memory of Nineveh was a very bitter one, and the thought that God could forgive its people would be totally unacceptable to many Jews, perhaps as difficult as the thought in our time that God might forgive the Nazis. One book in the Hebrew scriptures, the Book of Nahum, is entirely devoted to glorying in the coming downfall of Nineveh. The Book of Jonah dares to explore the limits of God's forgiveness and the thorny question it raises. Jonah literally does not want to live in a world in which people who commit such atrocities can get off scot-free just because they repent, but it seems that that is God's way. The gentleness with which God conveys this message to Jonah, and the fact that the book ends with a question mark, suggest that the writer means to raise this highly emotive issue in a tentative rather than confrontational way.

This question of the scandal of divine forgiveness is raised in some of the teaching of Jesus. In one of the most moving of his parables (Luke 15:11-32) a son persuades his father to let him have his share of the inheritance now rather than after the father's death. He then goes off and lives a riotous life until he becomes destitute. Eventually he swallows his pride and comes home to ask his father for a job on the farm, but his father welcomes him with open arms and throws a party to celebrate his return. The elder son, who has stayed at home and worked hard in the meantime, resents this, but the father insists that celebration is in order because "this brother of yours was dead and has come to life; he was lost and he has been found". Jesus told this story to justify the accusation that he was associating with the wrong kind of people (Luke 15:1-2), and so we are obviously meant to side with the father's point of view. However, it does not take much imagination to appreciate the feelings of the older brother. His argument is very much like that of those honest, hard-working, thrifty people of today who complain that people who spend their money recklessly end up being cushioned by the welfare state at the expense of the tax-payer. This resentment is quite natural, but we have to face the fact that being fair to everybody and at the same time compassionate towards those in real need is always a controversial matter, and sometimes a very emotive one.

Another parable (Matt 20:1-15) tells of a vineyard owner who hired workers for his harvest, some in the early morning, some at mid-day and some in the last hour before sunset. At the end of the day he paid them all the standard daily wage. This too sounds grossly unfair: no trade union would stand for it. And yet, what was to become of the families of those workers who had only had a few hours' employment if they were to be paid only a fraction of a day's wage, not enough to provide a supper for their families? In fact, unfair as this story may have seemed at the time, it is reflected in most developed countries today where the welfare system ensures that very thing: people are paid enough to live on whether they are employed or not. It is a matter of common humanity, but this does not deter some people from labelling the unemployed as "scroungers" and complaining of the unfairness of it all.

In the real world the balancing of justice with compassion is never simple. Justice can sometimes be lacking in compassion, and compassion can sometimes be seen as subverting justice. The biblical writers wrestled with this question as much as we do.

Justice and love tend to be seen as opposite poles in a portrait of the character of God. When the more liberally minded lay great stress on the love of God, more conservative believers are often heard to say, "Ah, but God is a God of justice as well". This dichotomy is quite false: justice is part of love. Real love is not just a soft feeling: it means caring about a person's welfare and acting in their best interest. As any parent knows, this often demands discipline and challenge. And as any parent of more than one child knows, the issue of fairness cannot be avoided. A preacher I once knew used to say that the birth of his first child taught him the meaning of love, and the birth of his second child taught him the meaning of justice. Justice is the practical working out of love when more than one person is involved. Moreover, there is a sentimental kind of compassion that can actually be offensive when it ignores the question of justice. We often hear today the complaint that those in the world who are poor and oppressed demand not "charity" but simple justice, putting right what is wrong, giving back to people the things that have been unjustly taken from them.

Real love can also have within it an element of anger. The "wrath" of God is an idea we tend to resist today, but that too is part of the Bible's portrayal of God as a real person. We may find in some Bible stories that it is somewhat arbitrary and extreme, that God seems to be wrathful about comparatively minor things, or over-sensitive about his own dignity like some insecure tyrant. However, genuine love surely means that we will be angry when we see cruelty and injustice being inflicted on people. Jesus, we are told, was angry when people quibbled about whether a disabled man should be cured on the Sabbath (Mark 3:5), and when his disciples turned children away from him (Mark 10:14).

"God is Love"

The reaching out for a loving God that we find in the Hebrew scriptures is intensified in the New Testament. All the Gospels tell how Jesus preached the primacy of love. When asked what the greatest commandment was, he quoted from Deuteronomy, "you shall love the Lord your God with all your heart, and with all your soul, and with all your mind, and with all your strength", and added to it the command from Leviticus, "You shall love your neighbour as yourself" (Mark 12:29-30, etc.; Deut 6:5; Lev 19:18). He added, according to Matthew: "On these two commandments hang all the law and the prophets" (Matt 22:40). We do not know that this was original to Jesus: it may well have already been a common teaching of the rabbis. According to Luke, it was a teacher of the law who quoted these words to Jesus rather than Jesus saying them to him (Luke 10:27). Moreover, it was the lawyer who actually quoted them together as one commandment.

However, the Gospels make it quite clear how radically Jesus interpreted the centrality of these commandments. The lawyer who quoted them to Jesus in Luke's Gospel asked "who is my neighbour?", and the response of Jesus was the story of the Good Samaritan, with its disturbing implication that the hated heretic Samaritan turned out to be a better neighbour than the good Jewish priest and Levite. In other places we find Jesus advocating love of enemies (Matt 5:44) and unlimited forgiveness (Matt 18:22), and putting reconciliation before religious ritual (Matt 5:23-24). In his actions, too, Jesus was constantly breaking through the barriers that divided people from one another, reaching out to those despised by the community.

Outside the Gospels, too, we find the primacy of love being asserted. Paul, often thought of quite wrongly as a dry theologian, emphasizes the love of God shown in Christ, saying such things as "God proves his love for us in that while we were sinners Christ died for us" (Rom 5:8) and asserting his conviction that nothing in all creation can separate us from "the love of God in Christ Jesus our Lord" (Rom 8:39). For Paul, the wellspring of the life of faith is that "God's love has been poured into our hearts through the Holy Spirit" (Rom 5:5). And it is of course to Paul that we owe the beautiful hymn to love with its statement that "if I have prophetic powers, and understand all mysteries and all knowledge, and if I have all faith, so as to remove mountains, but do not have love, I am nothing" (1 Cor 13:2). This leaves us in no doubt as to what Paul, with all his talk of prophecy, knowledge and faith, regarded as the central thing.

The writings under the name of John (though we do not know whether or not they come from the same person) have their own slant on this theme of love. In the Gospel of John there is a particular sense of intimacy between Jesus and his disciples. The account of the supper on the evening before his crucifixion begins by saying that "having loved his own who were in the world, he loved them to the end". He then goes on to wash his disciples' feet, and after the supper he says, "I give you a new commandment, that you love one another" (John 13). It is in John's Gospel that we find the mysterious character of "the disciple whom Jesus loved" (John 13:23 etc.), and the threefold challenge to Peter after the Resurrection: "Simon, son of John, do you love me?" (John 21:15-17).

It is in the first Epistle of John that we find the ultimate expression of the centrality of love in the simple, absolute statement: "God is love" (1 John 4:7,16). This is followed up with its implication: that no one, no matter what their spirituality, theological knowledge or religious credentials may be, can know God at all unless they love, and that anyone who genuinely lives in love lives in God. As we have seen, there is much in the Bible that breathes an atmosphere very different from this, yet this seems to be the fundamental quest of the Bible writers as it is of many of us today – a God of love to believe in, and the experience of living our lives in love.

9

Is There Life After Death?

"Who knows whether the human spirit goes upwards and the spirit of animals goes downwards to the earth?"
(Eccles 3:21)

Most religions are concerned with the question of what is beyond this life. "What happens when we die?" is often the question that first prompts people to start thinking about God or spirituality.

The issue is raised in the Bible as early as the second and third chapters. It is not clear from the story whether or not Adam and Eve were meant to be immortal but became mortal because of their disobedience. This was read into it by later interpreters, notably the apostle Paul, when he contrasted Jesus with Adam: "just as sin came into the world through one man, and death came through sin..." (Rom 5:12). The story itself, like so much else in the Bible, is deeply ambiguous. God had warned Adam and Eve not to eat the fruit of the tree of the knowledge of good and evil because "in the day that you eat of it you shall die" (Gen 2:17), but they did not die that day. Instead, they were told that their life would be hard, and they were reminded of the reality of ultimate death: "you are dust, and to dust you shall return" (Gen 3:19).

The stories later in Genesis seem to deliberately contrast the shortness of human life with the eternity of God. The genealogy from Adam to Noah (Gen 5) is a list of people who lived impossibly long lives. However, there is probably significance in the fact that most of them lived a little over nine hundred years. Perhaps the point being made here is that no human has ever lived for a thousand years – that is a length of time associated only with God. Psalm 90 is more realistic about human life, saying: "the days of our life are seventy years, or perhaps eighty, if we are strong", but reminding us that to God a thousand years are "like yesterday when it is passed, or like a watch in the night". The implication it draws from this is the prayer: "So teach us to number our days, that we may apply our hearts unto wisdom".

The Israelite View of Death

Generally, the writers of the Hebrew scriptures did not rebel against the fact of death as such. They saw it as a natural part of being a creature. They thought that the dead, in so far as they existed at all, lived in a shadowy underworld cut off from the living and from God. Untimely death was certainly a tragedy; to be left unburied, eaten by birds and animals, was even worse; but death in old age was simply the natural end of life. It is said of Abraham that he "breathed his last and died in a good old age, an old man and full of years, and was gathered to his people" (Gen 25:8). A similar expression is used of Ishmael (Gen 25:17), Jacob (Gen 49:29) and others. Moses, one of the greatest of men, "whom the LORD knew face to face" is not said to have gone to Heaven: he simply died and was buried in an unknown grave (Deut 34:5-6.10). Of David it is said that he "slept with his fathers" (1 Kgs 2:10, AV). The same is said of his son Solomon (1 Kgs 11:43) and other kings.

There were only a few exceptions to this. In the early part of Genesis we find the character of Enoch, of whom it is said that he "walked with God; then he was no more, because God took him" at the comparatively young age (in the context of that genealogy) of three hundred and sixty five (Gen 5:24). This led to a later idea that Enoch was somehow immortal and able to impart knowledge of the future to later generations. Around the time of the birth of Christianity, several popular apocalyptic writings appeared under the name of Enoch.

Of Elijah, who was considered in some ways as the father of

prophecy, it is said that he was caught up into Heaven by a whirlwind (2 Kgs 2:11). Of him too, it was believed that he was still alive in Heaven and would return to prepare the people for the final "day of the LORD" (Mal 4:5). John the Baptist, as the forerunner of Jesus, was thought by some to be the returned Elijah (Matt 17:10-13).

Another sort of exception is found in the story of how King Saul, at a time of desperation, asked a witch to call up the spirit of the deceased Samuel to give him advice (1 Sam 28). Samuel came up out of the ground as an old man wrapped in a robe, and his first words to Saul were "Why have you disturbed me by bringing me up?" The whole procedure was frowned upon by Israelite religion. The irony was that Saul had come to the medium in disguise, because he himself had expelled all "the mediums and the wizards" from the land.

The psalmists see death as the end of their relationship with God. One of them, presumably in sickness or danger, asks what profit it will be to God to allow him to die: "Will the dust praise you? Will it tell of your faithfulness?" (Ps 30:9; cf. Ps 88:11-12). Another psalm distinguishes between three realms in relation to God: "The heavens are the LORD's heavens, but the earth he has given to human beings. The dead do not praise the LORD, nor do any that go down into silence. But we will bless the LORD from this time on and for evermore" (Ps 115:17-18). It is clear from the context that "for evermore" is an expression for the whole of life, or perhaps for generations to come, but does not imply that those speaking will continue praising God after they die.

The prophet of Isaiah 65, painting a word picture of a future Jerusalem richly blessed, says: "one who dies at a hundred years will be considered a youth, and one who falls short of a hundred years will be considered accursed" (Is 63:20). The assumption is that in an ideal world everyone would enjoy a long, healthy life, but even in that world death would not be eliminated.

The people behind the Hebrew scriptures saw themselves as

part of the ongoing process of life on this earth. It was through their descendants that they thought of themselves as living for ever. To have children was very important. A good life, blessed by God, could be summed up thus: "You shall know that your descendants will be many and your offspring like the grass of the earth. You shall come to your grave in ripe old age, as a shock of grain comes up to the threshing-floor in its season" (Job 5:25-26).

The well-loved twenty-third Psalm is often read at funerals because of its apparent assurance of everlasting life: "Yea, though I walk through the valley of the shadow of death, I will fear no evil... and I will dwell in the house of the LORD forever". Here too, however, we have to understand what the expressions mean. The first one is a Hebrew way of talking of a deep, dark valley. The image of the shepherd is still uppermost here: the sheep passing through a frighteningly dark valley is reassured by the shepherd's protecting rod and staff. By the end of the psalm the image has changed from God as a shepherd to God as a generous host preparing a table for his guest, anointing his head and filling his wine cup to overflowing. Dwelling in the house of the Lord signifies living in the constant presence of God, and the phrase translated "forever" is literally "for length of days": the New Revised Standard Version translates it "my whole life long".

Another passage in the Hebrew scriptures often quoted as referring to life after death is the one found in the Book of Job and immortalized in Handel's *Messiah*. We quote it, as Handel does, from the King James Version, showing the words that version puts in italics as a sign that they are not in the original Hebrew:

"For I know *that* my redeemer liveth, and *that* he shall stand at the latter day upon the earth: and *though* after my skin *worms* destroy this *body*, yet in my flesh shall I see God: whom I shall see for myself, and mine eyes shall behold, and not another" (Job 19:25-27).

The number of italicized words shows how very obscure and ambiguous this passage is. Even its translation has been overlaid with centuries of later Jewish and Christian interpretation. The New Revised Standard Version, like all versions, struggles to make better sense of it. Including the marginal notes, it reads:

> "For I know that my Redeemer (*or, Vindicator*) lives, and that at the last he (*or, that he the Last*) will stand upon the earth (*or, dust*); and after my skin has been thus destroyed, then in (*or, without*) my flesh I shall see God (*meaning of Heb of this verse uncertain*), whom I shall see on my side (*or, for myself*)"

This translation makes it even more obvious how unclear the meaning is. Its main theme seems to be that Job will one day see his "Redeemer". This word (*go'el* in Hebrew) denotes the person who is responsible for someone: what we would call the "next of kin". The *go'el* is the one who may be called upon to pay your debts, to redeem you from bonded labour, or to act as your advocate in standing up for your rights. This last meaning is what seems to be the one here. Job, suffering physically and being branded a sinner by his "comforters", asserts that in the end God will turn out to be his advocate. However, whether this means after he has died, or simply after his skin has been destroyed by the disease he is suffering, is not at all clear.

Raising from the dead is not unknown in the Hebrew scriptures. The story is told (1 Kgs 17:17-24) of Elijah reviving a young lad when "there was no breath left in him". It is not quite clear whether the boy was literally dead or whether Elijah gave him a kind of "kiss of life" when he was at the point of death. However, in the similar story told about Elisha (2 Kgs 4:18-37) it is quite clear that the child is already dead when his mother sends for the prophet. These exceptional stories do not alter the fact that the ancient Hebrews regarded death as final, and as part of the God-given order of things. Even someone who had been miraculously raised from death would die a natural death eventually.

Hope in the Living God

This is not to say that there is no concept of resurrection in the Hebrew scriptures. The Israelites believed in a God who is almighty, and who is Lord of life and death. They saw the natural cycle of the seasons as a sign of the victory of life over death. This comes out, for instance, in Psalm 104, which says to God in reference to all living creatures: "When you take away their breath, they die and return to their dust. When you send forth your spirit (or, breath), they are created, and you renew the face of the ground" (Ps 104:29-30). Job recognizes that a tree that is cut down can renew itself even it seems to have died, but acknowledges that this does not happen to human beings (Job 14:7-12).

This image of a tree appears also in the Book of Isaiah, where the prophet describes a future king as "a shoot... from the stock of Jesse" (Is 11:1). The implication is that though the line of David may be hopelessly corrupted or even extinct, there will be a new start from the very roots. It will be as when God sent the prophet Samuel to the house of Jesse to find the chosen king (1 Sam 16). Here it is not the resurrection of a dead individual that is in view, but the resurrection of a dead dynasty: a sign that whatever happens God is faithful to his ancient promises and can do something new.

This restoration of life in a dead situation is a strong theme throughout the Hebrew scriptures. The whole story of the people begins with the promise of innumerable descendants to Abraham, though he and his wife Sarah are old and childless. As the New Testament Letter to the Hebrews comments: "from one person, and this one as good as dead, descendants were born, as many as the stars of heaven" (Heb 11:12). This theme of unpromising beginnings is frequently repeated. Jacob and Esau were born to Rebekah when she had appeared for a long time to be incapable of bearing children (Gen 25:21). Later, when the descendants of Abraham had been slaves in Egypt for a long time, the Exodus came as a kind of resurrection. This too had unpromising beginnings. It was brought about through Moses, who had narrowly escaped death as a baby, had fled from Egypt in disgrace as an adult, and who in his own eyes was unsuitable for the task because he was such a poor speaker (Ex 3:10). The great leader Samuel, who presided over the birth of the monarchy, was the child of a woman who for years was despised by her husband's other wife because she seemed incapable of having children (1 Sam 1). The same motif continues into the New Testament, where John the Baptist is born of an elderly childless couple, and Jesus is born of a virgin.

In the Book of Ezekiel we find a vision of resurrection. The prophet is led into a valley full of dry bones, like the site of a battle where a huge army has been defeated. God asks him, "Can these bones live?", to which he replies, "O Lord GOD, you know". Then there is a great noise of rattling, and the bones come together into bodies, flesh and sinews grow on them, and the wind blows breath into them. This is a vision of the restoration of the Jewish nation and its return from Babylon to its own land. God says, "I am going to open your graves, and bring you up from your graves, O my people. I will put my spirit within you, and you shall live" (Ezek 37:1-14). It is doubtful that the prophet literally thought that dead Jews would be restored to life. The story is more likely to have been a vivid image of the restoration of the people.

The joy, and the challenge, of this renewal is seen in the words of the "second Isaiah": "Do not remember the former things, or consider the things of old. I am about to do a new thing" (Is 43:18-19).

And so, although the people behind the Hebrew scriptures

did not generally imagine the survival of individuals after death, their faith in a living, powerful God led them to believe that, however bad the situation, there could always be a new beginning. This belief at least contained the seed of what became faith in the Resurrection. In fact, there is one passage in the Book of Isaiah which takes us to the threshold of this. Anticipating the restoration of the people after defeat by their enemies, the prophet dreams of a great feast being spread "for all peoples", and says that God "will swallow up death forever" and "wipe away the tears from all faces" (Is 25:6-8).

The assumption that there was no life for the individual after death met its starkest challenge in the second century BCE. When the Syrian king Antiochus Epiphanes was trying to stamp out the Jewish way of life and the Maccabean rebels were fighting to save it, thousands of young men were killed while defending their faith. There was no way in which these young men could be said to have been rewarded for their faithfulness – there had to be some judgment and vindication beyond this present life. The Book of Daniel, which was probably written around this time, says: "Many of those who sleep in the dust of the earth shall awake, some to everlasting life, and some to shame and everlasting contempt" (Dan 12:2).

In the Apocryphal Book of Wisdom we find the firm assertion that the righteous who die go to a more glorious heavenly life: "But the souls of the righteous are in the hand of God, and no torment will ever touch them. In the eyes of the foolish they seemed to have died, and their departure was thought to be a disaster, and their going from us to be their destruction; but they are at peace. For though in the sight of others they were punished, their hope is full of immortality" (Wisd 3:1-4).

This belief was apparently current at the time of the writing of Ecclesiastes, but the writer of this very sceptical book questions it: "For the fate of humans and the fate of animals are the same; as one dies, so dies the other... Who knows whether the human spirit goes upwards and the spirit of animals goes downwards to the earth?" (Eccles 3:19-21)

By New Testament times belief in the resurrection of the dead had become more common among the Jews, but the Sadducees still disputed it, probably because they had a more conservative view of the Hebrew scriptures and would not accept ideas that had developed in more recent times. The Pharisees believed in it, and Jesus seems to have sided with them on this issue. Granted such a belief, the big question was the nature of the resurrection life. Some Sadducees taunted Jesus with the hypothetical situation of a woman who had been married successively to seven men, and posed the question "in the resurrection whose wife will she be?" Jesus responded by saying that the resurrection life is not like this one. There will be no marriage there. Those who partake of the resurrection life will be like the angels in Heaven (Matt 22:23-32 etc.).

Jesus' parable about the rich man and the poor man Lazarus (Luke 16:19-31) pictures Lazarus after death being carried away by the angels to rest in Abraham's bosom: a vivid picture of the old phrase "he was gathered to his people". The rich man meanwhile was being tormented in the flames of Hell. Another parable (Matt 25:31-46) pictures the judgment of the nations as a separation of the sheep from the goats. The Son of Man will judge them according to the way they have treated the least of his brothers when they were in need. Those who showed mercy will go into eternal life, while those who have not will go to eternal punishment.

The question of whether eternal punishment in the flames of Hell is consistent with a loving God is one about which Christians have argued for centuries, and we have to question what Jesus meant in parables like this. We must take into account that Jesus' preaching was in the tradition of the prophets, and that prophetic preaching often deals in vivid, dramatic imagery. It is also worth noting that the idea of Hell, so often used in

Christian preaching to frighten ordinary people into a way of life approved by their "betters", is always used by Jesus to the opposite effect, as a warning to the rich and powerful about the way they treat the poor.

The Gospel of the Resurrection

The Christian church declared from the beginning that Jesus had risen from the dead, but to ascertain what exactly was meant by this is difficult. The nearest we have to a description of the event is what seems to be a highly dramatized account in Matthew's Gospel, where it is said that there was a great earthquake and an angel of the Lord descended from Heaven and rolled back the stone that covered the tomb (Matt 28:2). But even here the actual coming of Jesus to life is not described.

Our earliest account of the Resurrection is that of Paul (1 Cor 15:3-8). Saying that he is passing on what was told to him, he says that Jesus "died for our sins according to the scriptures", that he was buried, and that he was raised on the third day. He then mentions the appearance to Cephas (Peter), then to "the twelve" (which, unless it was a slip of the tongue, suggests that he did not know about Judas). Then, he says, Jesus appeared to more than five hundred at once, then to James, then to all the apostles, and finally to himself. This suggests that Paul had been given an oft-repeated list of the evidences for the Resurrection, and then added his own experience to the list, but strangely there is no mention of the empty tomb that figures so largely in the four Gospels. One wonders whether this is an imaginative embellishment that emerged later, or a story that had been suppressed because people were reluctant to take into account the evidence of women.

There is also an ambiguity about the nature of the Resurrection appearances. Luke tells the story of two disciples (only one of whom is named) meeting a stranger on the road to Emmaus who explained the meaning of the death of Jesus in the light of the scriptures. It was only when they sat down to supper with him and he gave thanks and broke the bread that they realised it was Jesus. The idea of their conversing so long with him and not recognising him is so unlikely that it suggests the story is not meant to be taken literally. It is more likely to be making the point that whenever and wherever disciples hear the scriptures expounded and break bread together the living Christ is with them.

The ending of Mark's Gospel is confused and mysterious. In the most ancient and reliable manuscripts the story breaks off rather abruptly at verse 8. Other manuscripts add further material which is fairly obviously derived from what is said in other Gospels. The only thing on which all manuscripts agree is that the women who visited the tomb saw a young man who told them that Jesus had been raised, and that they ran away in terror and amazement and were afraid to tell anyone about it.

While Luke's account in the Gospel and in Acts says that Jesus appeared to his disciples during a period of forty days and then ascended into Heaven, Paul talks of his experience on the Damascus road years later as a Resurrection appearance in the same category as the others. This is described in Acts (9:3-9) as a flashing light that temporarily blinded him, accompanied by the voice of Jesus speaking to him. His companions heard the voice but saw no one. Later, when Paul tells the story to the crowd in Jerusalem, he says that his companions saw the light but did not hear the voice (Acts 22:9). In a later account still (Acts 26:12-18) Paul relates a longer speech of Jesus to him, but in none of the accounts does it say that Paul actually *saw* Jesus.

And so the whole story of the Resurrection, which is so central to the earliest proclamation of the Christian message, is shrouded in mystery and ambiguity. We cannot be sure what exactly the early Christians meant by saying "The Lord is risen", or whether they necessarily all meant the same thing.

They certainly believed that they would share the resurrection life of Jesus, but this too was expressed in different and sometimes inconsistent ways. The popular conception in Christian culture today and indeed for many centuries back, is that the soul leaves the body at death and goes to Heaven, so that those we have loved and lost are alive in a better world, and we shall be re-united with them when we die. This is believed in spite of the way Jesus implied that there is no marriage in Heaven. It is also thought that those who have died are in the presence of God and at the same time still in touch with the world. In fact, Catholic tradition lays great stress on asking the saints in Heaven to pray for us.

All these ideas are really expressions of the immortality of the soul, a belief that is not basically biblical, but derived from Greek philosophy and Eastern religions. In Hebrew thinking, a human being was not a soul in a body but a single being who could only be either alive or dead. The idea of a disembodied human being had no place in this thinking. That is why in parts of the New Testament we find the belief that that those who have died remain dead until the end of the world, when everybody who has ever lived will be raised to life for the final judgment and then consigned to Heaven or Hell. This is the picture in the Book of Revelation (Rev 20:12-15), which talks of the sea giving up its dead, echoing Daniel's vision of those who "sleep in the dust of the earth" being awakened (Dan 12:2)..

However, there seem to be different views within the New Testament itself, perhaps because of the merging of some Greek ideas with the traditional Hebrew conception. Luke's Gospel has Jesus saying to the thief on the cross, "today you will be with me in paradise" (Luke 23:43). Here again we must beware of assuming that the Bible gives one final answer. The early Christians were attempting to come to terms with the new sense of hope and victory they had found in their experience of Jesus, and naturally they expressed it in different ways. All these ways were in a sense picture language rather than theories about what is the case.

Paul's first Letter to the Thessalonians, which is probably the earliest complete book in the New Testament, was written at a time when the return of Christ in glory was expected to happen in the very near future. The Christians in Thessalonica were puzzled because some of their number had died. Would they miss the glorious appearance of Jesus on which they had pinned their hopes? Paul reassures them that there is no fear of this. When Jesus returns from Heaven to the sound of God's trumpet, he says, the dead will be raised. In fact, they will have priority and "we who are alive, who are left, will be caught up in the clouds together with them to meet the Lord in the air" (1 Thess 4:13-18). This apparently very realistic and literal expectation is echoed in Paul's discussion of the Resurrection in his first Letter to the Corinthians. Again there is the sound of a trumpet, and "the dead will be raised imperishable, and we will be changed". Paul still expects that many believers, including himself, will still be alive when Christ returns, and that both the dead and the living will acquire a new form of being: "for this perishable body must put on imperishability, and this mortal body must put on immortality" (1 Cor 15:51-53).

However, in his second Letter to the Corinthians (4:7 – 5:10) Paul expresses the hope of resurrection in a different way. First, he stresses that the life-giving power of Christ is already present in us, counteracting the forces of death. In all our sufferings we are "carrying in the body the death of Jesus, so that the life of Jesus may be made visible in our mortal flesh". We have Christ within us like a treasure in common clay jars, giving us a life with two aspects, in which "even though our outer nature is wasting away, our inner nature is being renewed day by day". This experience is all a matter of faith, looking not to the temporal things that can be seen but to the eternal things that cannot be seen. He talks of death as the destruction of "the earthly tent we live in" and its replacement by "a building from God, a house not made with hands, eternal in the heavens", so that we can look forward to being "away from the body and at home with the Lord". This is closer to the Greek conception of the soul as an entity that can exist in the absence of the body.

When Paul became a prisoner with serious charges against him, and realised that he himself could die soon, he seems to have become more aware that whatever happened to his body his soul was free. Writing to the Philippians, he admits that he is torn between the desire to "depart and be with Christ" on the one hand and his feeling on the other hand that the needs of the church will best be met by his remaining "in the body" (Phil 1:20-26).

And so, rather than a clear, consistent doctrine, what we find in the Bible is the expression of the hopes, dreams and thoughts of many people about the ultimate mystery of what happens after we die and, in the New Testament, their attempts to express the sense of the victory of life over death in Jesus. On this issue, as on others, there are two "stories" which seem to be inconsistent with each other. One is that the body will die and be restored at the end of time, and the other is that when we die we leave the body and are in the immediate presence of Christ.

In the New Testament generally, however, the hope of resurrection was not the rather private, personal thing that it often is today. The focus was not generally on the destiny of the individual, but on the transformation of the whole world when God's purpose through Christ would be finally accomplished. The concern of people who had lost friends and relatives through death was not whether they would personally meet them again, but whether those who had died would miss the glorious event that was about to happen for the whole world.

As time went by, and Christians began to realise that perhaps this event was not as imminent as they thought, the focus shifted towards a sense of "eternal life" being a quality of life here and now which would not end with death. This is particularly stressed in John's Gospel, where sometimes it is suggested that the "coming again" of Jesus is the presence of the Spirit in and among believers: "In a little while the world will no longer see me, but you will see me; because I live, you also will live... Those who love me will keep my word, and my Father will love them, and we will come to them and make our home with them" (John 14:19,23). At the same time it is said that Jesus, in ascending into Heaven, was going to "prepare a place" for his followers, "so that where I am, there you may be also" (John 14:2-3). However, the focus is not on our reunion with each other, but on being with Jesus and being like him. The first Letter of John (1 John 3:2) says: "Beloved, we are God's children now; what we will be has not yet been revealed. What we do know is this: when he is revealed, we will be like him, for we will see him as he is."

The Gospel of John also gives us the story of the raising of Lazarus, and the saying of Jesus that is always used at funerals, usually in the words of the King James Bible: "I am the resurrection and the life: he that believeth in me, though he were dead, yet shall he live: and whosoever liveth and believeth in me shall never die" (John 11:25-26). These words have comforted mourners down through the generations, but which of us if challenged could explain what they really mean? Like so much that is in the Bible, the hope of eternal life is elusive, indefinable and open-ended.

Popular spirituality today has absorbed elements that are not generally found in the Bible, especially the idea of reincarnation. Though it derives mainly from Hinduism and Buddhism via "New Age" thinking, many Christians too go along with the idea that when we die our soul will go into another body and live a life as someone else. Some people believe they can actually recall past lives. The idea is an attractive one: why should this life be the only one? Even if we believe in an eternal life after we die, why should what we do in this one short life be final in deciding where we spend eternity? Even among many Christians who believe in judgment, there is a feeling that it would be much fairer if God were to give us "another go". However, Christians have usually resisted this belief because of its implication that this world is unreal. It implies that we are essentially souls, not attached permanently to one body or even perhaps to one planet, and that reality is centred not in this world but somewhere "out there" in a non-physical realm.

As we have seen, there are elements of this kind of thinking about "body" and "soul" in the New Testament. There are even suggestions of reincarnation. Some people said that John the Baptist was Elijah (Matt 17:13), while some said that Jesus was John the Baptist, Elijah, or "Jeremiah or one of the prophets" (Matt 16:14). However, there is throughout the Bible a very strong sense of the unity of the physical creation, and of a human being as an integral whole rather than a soul living in a body. The people who produced the Hebrew scriptures hoped to live on through their children. The prophets looked to the establishment of a right society in this world. Even though this might have consequences for the whole realm of nature, the vision is not of the annihilation of the earth or its being absorbed into Heaven, but of "a new heaven and a new earth" (Is 65:17; Rev 21:1). As for us human beings, the belief usually expressed is that we will rise again to live on a new earth with a new, incorruptible body (1 Cor 15:42-44). This will be not a pure spirit, but a "spiritual body". There is a strong belief among the biblical writers that the God who created us as living bodies is able to take that life away and give it back to us: death is the end of human life, but God can create a new beginning.

Another popular idea that is different from the biblical conception is that death is only a peaceful transition from one mode of existence to another. The poem "Death is nothing at all", written by Henry Scott Holland more than a century ago, has become enormously popular as a funeral reading in recent years. However, it is very far removed from the attitude of most of the people who contributed to the Bible. For them, death was a grim reality, a real end. Though it might be natural after a long life, it was a sad necessity involving pain and trouble (Ps 90:10), and if it was untimely it was a thoroughly bad thing. The only hope beyond it was of a miracle brought about by the power of God.

Unlike many of the Gnostics in the early days, and Muslims later, mainline Christian faith has always emphasized that the death of Jesus was real. The Apostles' Creed seems determined that there should be no doubt about it. Jesus, it says, "was crucified, dead, and buried. He descended into hell. On the third day (the implication being "not until then") he rose again from the dead". Although John's Gospel represents Jesus as saying of his life "I have authority to lay it down and authority to take it up again" (John 10:18), the general message of the New Testament is not that Jesus "rose" but that he "was raised". Being dead, he had no power in himself to rise again: it was God who raised him.

This is the spirituality of faith and hope rather than of knowledge and understanding. It arises out of the conception of a living, personal God with whom we can have a relationship, someone we can appeal to, someone we can trust even when everything seems to be against us. It is not so much the spirituality of *insight*, of seeing the inner meaning behind the outward one, as a spirituality of *paradox*, or even *irony*. Just as the psalmists, and many modern Jews, can say that everything is as bad as it can be, but God is good, so the faith of the New Testament could assert that death is real and final, but life has the victory.

10

Beyond the Ordinary

*"... someone who becomes a terrorist and someone who goes to a U2
concert have something in common. They both want to escape from
the materialistic, dull daily life. You see what I mean? Both are
looking for transcendence."*
(Bono)[1]

*"Ah, but a man's reach should exceed his grasp,
Or what's a heaven for?"*
Robert Browning, *Andrea del Sarto*

The rather disturbing juxtaposition of terrorism and a rock
concert as signs of the quest for transcendence is surprisingly
close to what we find in the Bible. The spiritual quest is in many
ways a desire for excitement. We human beings tend never to be
content with simply surviving. Even those people in the world
who have to struggle for the basic necessities of food and shelter
look for something to lift them out of that struggle if only for a
moment – music, dancing, religious ceremonies, games, alcohol
or drugs. The majority of us in the West, who have our basic
needs amply met, still crave something more. Children get up to
mischief just for the fun of it. Teenagers hanker after fast motor-
bikes, loud music and wild parties. Older people are passionate
about their hobbies, obsessed with possessions as marks of
status, or transported with the wonder of great art and music.
Some turn to drink or drugs in order to experience feelings that
seem to be unavailable in their ordinary life – a feeling of ecstasy
or of being "high". Most people fall in love at some time or other,
while many dream of falling in love, or settle for the more
immediate excitement of casual sex. Excitement, adventure,

ecstasy, dreams, romance: all these are a vital part of what it means to be human, and they can be expressed in a thousand ways.

Religion and spirituality are part of this. They are ways of seeking an enhanced consciousness, a stronger sense of being alive, a feeling of being part of something bigger than oneself. Religion in many cultures has included the use of drugs to induce an extra-ordinary state of mind. Music, too, often has that function. Something like this appears in a story in the Bible (1 Sam 10), where the future King Saul meets a band of "prophets" coming down from the sanctuary with "harp, tambourine, flute and lyre". He joins with them in their "prophetic frenzy" and is "turned into a different person". The way in which the story is told suggests that these "prophets" were rather looked down upon and mocked by many people, but it may be that in early Israel they were considered to receive messages from God when in that state of mind. There are charismatic Christian churches where this kind of experience is present, but similar phenomena appear in some part of most religious traditions.

On a more conventional level, the feeling of exaltation experienced by large assemblies is a universal phenomenon. Whether in the loud singing and hand-clapping of a charismatic church, an old-fashioned Nonconformist congregation singing hymns, or dignified sung Mass in a great cathedral with a professional choir, the feeling of being "lifted up" is a fundamental part of spirituality. This is just as true in situations that are not overtly religious – a political rally, a football match, the last night of the London Proms or, as Bono's remark above suggests, a rock concert. At a concert like that large numbers of people gather for a life-affirming experience. It is often not just a common appreciation of a certain kind of music they are celebrating, but a common set of beliefs and values. They have come together to celebrate and reinforce those beliefs and values, and in this respect a concert can function as a kind of religious service.

There is much of this in the Bible, concentrated mainly in the Book of Psalms. With examples like Ps 95 ("O come, let us sing to the LORD; let us make a joyful noise to the rock of our salvation") and many others, including the final psalm (Ps 150) that exhorts people to praise God with trumpet, lute, harp, tambourine and dance, strings and pipe and "loud clashing cymbals" and concludes with "Let everything that breathes praise the LORD! Praise the LORD!" we are left in no doubt that worship in ancient Israel could be a very joyful experience, lifting people out of their ordinary day-to-day existence.

Psalm 42 is a lament expressing this desire for the sanctuary by someone who is far away and "cast down" in spirit: "As a deer longs for flowing streams, so my soul longs for you, O God... When shall I come and behold the face of God?... These things I remember, as I pour out my soul: how I went with the throng, and led them in procession to the house of God, with glad shouts and songs of thanksgiving, a multitude keeping festival".

In ancient Israel, and in the thoughts of dispersed Jews centuries later, the Temple in Jerusalem had a special place. Even today Jews stand at the Wailing Wall to lament its loss. Some psalms express the joy of pilgrims as they approached the Holy City: "Great is the LORD and greatly to be praised in the city of our God. His holy mountain, beautiful in elevation, is the joy of all the earth" (Ps 48:1-2). The joy of arriving is expressed in another psalm: "I was glad when they said to me, 'Let us go to the house of the LORD!' Our feet are standing within your gates, O Jerusalem" (Ps 122:1-2).

Another aspect of this quest for the transcendent is the exalting of certain persons and institutions. We see it in displays of patriotism or in the pageantry of royal occasions. National pride (like religion according to Marx) can be the opium of the masses. In nineteenth century Britain many people working long hours in appalling conditions for little reward no doubt found some consolation in feeling that they were citizens of the greatest empire in the world, and turning out to wave their flags if ever Queen Victoria visited their town.

The biblical descriptions of the lavish abundance of King Solomon's court, of his ivory throne overlaid with the finest gold, of silver in his kingdom being as common as stones, and so on (1 Kgs 10:14-29; 2 Chr 11:13-28), are an expression of the pride and nostalgia that warmed the hearts of people living in later times when Judah was a small, poor state or perhaps even no longer a state at all. The king in Jerusalem was of course more than just wealthy and powerful – he was sacred, as we see in some of the psalms. He was the son of God (Ps 2:7), specially anointed and blessed (Ps 45), and destined to rule the earth (Ps 72:8).

Perhaps it is significant that in Western societies today, where patriotism and royalty are less universally valued than they once were, the cult of "celebrities" has reached extremes. No-one can entirely resist the thrill of meeting a famous person, even if that person, in the words of Andy Warhol, is only famous for fifteen minutes!

The Quest for Holiness

Majestic architecture and music, colourful vestments and ritual, and the gathering of large numbers of people, are all part of the enhancement of life and consciousness provided by public religion, but there can be a similar life-enhancing experience in private devotion. People often practise prayer or meditation with a view to being lifted into a higher state of consciousness, a feeling which they interpret as close communion with God, or with the depths of being.

The Jewish scriptures generally do not major on mysticism: for the ancient Israelites, as for most religious Jews today, the focus was mostly on practical action in obedience to the commandments. There is, however, evidence of a tradition of meditation on scripture. The laws of God are perceived as in themselves a source of joy. Psalm 19 combines what could be a very ancient hymn to the sun with a hymn to the law of God. It begins: "The heavens are telling the glory of God, and the firmament proclaims his handiwork". It then dwells for a few verses on the wonder of the cycle of day and night and the movement of the sun across the sky. But then the subject changes: "The law of the LORD is perfect, reviving the soul". Talking of the commandments of God it says: "More to be desired are they than gold, even much fine gold; sweeter also than honey, and drippings of the honeycomb".

Psalm 119, known chiefly for its extreme length, is an elaborate acrostic poem which has something of the labour of love about it. This love comes out here and there in direct statements like: "I find my delight in your commandments, because I love them. I revere your commandments, which I love, and I will meditate on your statutes" (Ps 119:47-48); "Oh, how I love your law! It is my meditation all day long!" (Ps 119:97); "How sweet are your words to my taste, sweeter than honey to my mouth!" (Ps 119:103).

Meditation on God's laws leads into a desire for holiness of life. Many religious people find in pursuing a holy life the kind of extra-ordinary experience others look for in pleasure, excitement and adventure, or in the more superficial aspects of community religion. There is an innate desire in human beings, perhaps shown more in some than in others, to be special, to be somehow different from the ordinary run of human beings. The Israelites as a nation saw themselves as a special people set apart in some way for God. God had said to them: "If you obey my voice and keep my covenant, you shall be my treasured possession out of all the peoples... you shall be for me a priestly kingdom and a holy nation" (Ex 19:5-6) This status involved certain patterns of behaviour. The Ten Commandments and all the other laws were an implication of being God's holy people.

This is especially stressed in the part of Leviticus that is often called "the Holiness Code" (Lev 17-26). Its overall theme is: "You shall be holy, for I the LORD your God am holy" (Lev 19:2). Much of this holiness is expressed as a matter of being distinct from other people. The Israelites must not follow the ways of the Egyptians from whom they have departed nor those of the Canaanites in the land they are to enter, but must live by the laws of their God (Lev 18:3-5). Many of the ritual laws, such as the prohibition on cutting the hair from one's temples, trimming the beard, making cuts in the flesh as a sign of mourning, or having tattoos (Lev 19:27-28; 21:1-5) were probably chiefly a matter of being different from surrounding nations. However, the Holiness Code also includes commandments with a much more universal ethical theme, concerned with respect for parents, the elderly, the blind and the deaf, hired workers, immigrants and all kinds of vulnerable people (Lev 19:13-14, 32-34 etc.). There are rules too about honesty and social justice (Lev 19:11, 15-18, 35-36 etc.), and provision for generosity (Lev 19:9-10) and for avoiding a situation in which some people get trapped into poverty while others grow rich (Lev 25). And so, while many of the rules of holiness seem ritualistic and unreasonable, there is a clear link between holiness and ethical behaviour. This is well expressed in Psalm 24: "Who shall ascend the hill of the LORD? And who shall stand in his holy place? Those who have clean hands and pure hearts, who do not lift up their souls to what is false, and do not swear deceitfully." (Ps 24:4)

All these commandments assumed extra importance after the Babylonian Exile. In fact, some of them were probably first formulated at that time. The prophets had interpreted the fall of Jerusalem as divine judgment on the unfaithfulness and impurity of the nation: it had failed to be truly the people of God. And so for many of the people in the Exile and afterwards purity, distinctiveness and obedience to God's law became all-important. The stories set in the time of the Exile, such as Daniel and his friends refusing to eat the unclean food provided for them in Babylon (Dan 1:8-21), Shadrach, Meshach and Abednego being thrown into a furnace for refusing to bow down to Nebuchadnezzar's statue (Dan 3), and Daniel locked up in the den of lions for praying to God instead of the Persian Emperor Darius (Dan 6), were designed to encourage Jews to take a courageous stand for the true God against the temptations of idolatry.

After the Exile, some of the Jewish leaders saw the idolatry and corruption of earlier times as the result of mingling with the other nations around and adopting aspects of their culture. And so the purity of the Jewish race came to acquire enormous importance. Ezra and Nehemiah, who re-constituted the Jewish community after the Exile, acted very rigorously to purge the people of the "sin" of intermarriage. Men who had married Gentiles were named and shamed, and instructed to turn their wives and children out (Ezra 10; Neh 13:23-29).

It is in actions like this that we begin to see the darker side of the quest for holiness. Deuteronomy presents Moses as telling the people that when they enter the Promised Land they must "utterly destroy" all the other inhabitants, showing them no mercy. They must on no account intermarry with them, but must "break down their altars, smash their pillars, hew down their sacred poles, and burn their idols with fire". This is what it means to be the holy people of God (Deut 7:1-6). The rules for warfare allow Israelites to capture and enslave defeated enemies of other countries, but when they defeat a town belonging to the people with whom they share the land of Canaan they "must not let anything that breathes remain alive" (Deut 20:16). These instructions were probably written and attributed to Moses during that post-exilic time when influential leaders like Ezra and Nehemiah were trying to purge the nation of all foreign influences. Perhaps from that time too comes the story of how, when King Saul defeated the Amalekites, it was held against him as a sin that he had spared Agag their king and kept some of their sheep and cattle instead of destroying them. Samuel the prophet came and denounced him, and then went and personally "hewed Agag in pieces before the LORD" (1 Sam 15:33).

The quest for the transcendent can lead to fanatical religion, to extreme self-righteousness and cruelty, as we see in religiously motivated terrorism today. It can even more easily degenerate into a discontent with being just human, a desire to be special and to feel spiritually superior to others. What begins as a spiritual aspiration can settle into the kind of complacency that actually loses all transcendence and becomes simple human pride: the sort of thing Jesus satirized in his portrait of the Pharisee saying his prayers: "God, I thank you that I am not like other people" (Luke 18:11).

Jesus and Holiness

Holiness in the sense of strict adherence to the divine Law had assumed great importance by the time of Jesus. Observance of the Sabbath, the holy day of rest, and of rules regarding what foods were "clean" or "unclean", together with rituals around the preparation of meat, ritual washing and so on were points on which the teachers of the Law often criticized Jesus and his disciples. The Pharisees were a numerous sect at the time. They believed in strict obedience to the Law in every detail. In the Gospels there are numerous accounts of disputes between Jesus and the Pharisees. While admiring their adherence to the divine law, he often denounced their attitudes and their behaviour. They criticized him for not being "holy": breaking the Sabbath, not strictly observing the rules about eating, and above all mingling freely with those labelled as "sinners" rather than keeping himself and his disciples separate from the sinful world.

This was a clash between two concepts of holiness. For the Pharisees, holiness meant protecting themselves from any possibility of being tainted by the unholy. The name "Pharisee" probably means something like "set apart". For Jesus, however, holiness meant emulating the character of God. He saw God not as keeping aloof from the world but as reaching out to everyone in love. To be holy means to share the nature of God, and for Jesus, since God's nature is universal love, this should be the chief measure of holiness. While Leviticus said "you shall be holy, for I the LORD your God am holy" (Lev 19:2), Jesus said "Love your enemies... so that you may be the children of your Father in heaven", and this to him was the way to "be perfect... as your heavenly Father is perfect" (Matt 5:43-48). Real holiness, according to Jesus, means being like God: open to the world and loving all people unconditionally. This kind of holiness, rather than being endangered or polluted by the world, can spread out and make the world itself holy.

The quest for transcendence in the Bible is not chiefly centred on the pursuit of personal sanctity. We have already seen how the quest for justice is a central theme in the Bible. This leads us into another dimension of transcendence, one that is more practical than some of these other paths and at the same time in a sense even more transcendent.

Notes

1. Michka Assayas, *Bono on Bono* (Hodder and Stoughton 2005, p 206)

11

The Dream of a New World

"For I am about to create new heavens and a new earth"
(Is 65:17)

Most people are familiar with the saying in the Book of Revelation, "Then I saw a new heaven and a new earth", partly because this passage is sometimes read at funerals with its comforting assurance: "And God shall wipe away all tears from their eyes; and there shall be no more death, neither sorrow, nor crying, neither shall there be any more pain: for the former things are passed away" (Rev 21:1,4).

However, few are aware that those words were inspired by the Book of Isaiah. It is interesting to compare Revelation 21 with Isaiah 65. They echo one another and yet are different. In the Isaiah passage the phrase "new heavens and a new earth" turns out as we read on to be a hyperbolic introduction to a very earthly vision of Jerusalem: not the New Jerusalem of Revelation that comes down from Heaven, but the actual earthly city. Evidently speaking at one of those many times when Jerusalem was in a sorry state, the prophet imagines how God will bless it in the future: "for I am about to create Jerusalem as a joy, and its people as a delight... no more shall the sound of weeping be heard in it, or the cry of distress" (Is 65:18-19).

There follows a description of a safe, happy and healthy Jerusalem that verges on the miraculous but does not lose sight of the normal limitations of life. There will be no infant mortality or untimely death. A person who dies at a hundred years old will be considered to have died young. The people will live securely in the houses they have built and eat the fruit of the vines they have planted instead of seeing others take over their homes and their land. Having begun with poetic exaggeration, the prophet returns to it. In this ideal Jerusalem "the wolf and the lamb shall feed together, the lion shall eat straw like the ox". There will be no hurting or destroying on the holy mountain of Zion. However, evil may not be completely eliminated. The serpent will still be there, but will no longer attack people with its poisonous bite: its food will be the dust (Is 65:17-25).

When the prophets saw things wrong in their society, they painted horrifying pictures of divine judgment in the form of war, famine and pestilence, but when they wanted to reassure the nation that God was about to restore it to favour they could equally well present a description of peace and prosperity. The general principle is outlined in the Book of Deuteronomy, which lists the blessings that will come with obedience: "Blessed shall you be in the city, and blessed shall you be in the field. Blessed shall be the fruit of your womb, the fruit of your ground, and the fruit of your livestock" (Deut 28:3-4). The passage promises peace, prosperity, victory over enemies and prestige among the nations. It then goes on to describe in mirror-image terms (but at much greater length!) the curses that will result from disobedience, and finally adds a promise that if, after suffering all these curses, the people call God to mind again and change their ways, they will be forgiven and restored.

Predictions like this are found everywhere in the prophetic writings, often in vivid and poetic terms. At the end of the Book of Amos (9:11-15) there is a prophecy of harvests so plentiful that the ploughmen going out to prepare the ground for sowing will find that the reapers from the previous year have not yet finished! The Book of Joel, which apparently comes from a time of famine caused by a plague of locusts, calls the people to pray and promises a time when "the threshing-floors shall be full of grain, the vats shall overflow with wine and oil". This recovery of material welfare will be accompanied by spiritual blessing. There will be an outpouring of the Spirit of God, so that "your sons and your daughters shall prophesy, your old men shall dream dreams, and your young men shall see visions", and even the lowest in society will be filled with the Spirit (Joel 2:23-29).

Nature and Humanity

The prophets were poets. Poets often portray the immediate situation in cosmic terms, seeing the whole world in terms of their own feelings, as when W H Auden, in his *Funeral Blues*, says:

> *"The stars are not wanted now: put out every one;*
> *Pack up the moon and dismantle the sun;*
> *Pour away the ocean and sweep up the wood.*
> *For nothing now can ever come to any good."*

Jeremiah, contemplating the devastation of the land by the Babylonian invaders, says:

> "I looked on the earth, and, lo, it was waste and void; and to the heavens, and they had no light... I looked, and, lo, there was no one at all, and all the birds of the air had fled. I looked, and, lo, the fruitful land was a desert, and all its cities were laid in ruins before the LORD, before his fierce anger" (Jer 4:23-26).

This description suggests not just a devastation of the land of Israel but a total undoing of the work of God in creation, a return to the time when the earth was "without form and void" and not even light had been created.

The positive visions too could involve the whole world. In the Book of Isaiah we find the prophecy of a future king who will be truly righteous, and the prophet sees peace spreading out not only to the whole kingdom but to the whole creation:

"The wolf shall live with the lamb, the leopard shall lie down with the kid, the calf and the lion and the fatling together, and a little child shall lead them... for the earth shall be full of the knowledge of the LORD as the waters cover the sea" (Is 11:1-9).

Some of this, as we have seen, is echoed in a much later part of Isaiah.

Also in Isaiah we see the vision of the Temple Mount in Jerusalem being exalted above all the mountains of the world and the nations streaming to it to learn God's ways, so that "they shall beat their swords into ploughshares, and their spears into pruning hooks; nation shall not lift up sword against nation, neither shall they learn war any more" (Is 2:4). The Book of Micah uses this same passage, and adds a beautiful vision of peace: "but they shall sit under their own vines and under their own fig trees, and no one shall make them afraid" (Mic 4:4)

The prophets saw a connection between the world of human beings and the world of nature. Human beings were meant to cooperate with God in creation. They were meant to plough the soil, to plant and to harvest. The creation story in Genesis 2 tells how God placed Adam in the garden of Eden "to till it and keep it" (Gen 2:15). The biblical writers did not have any sentimental "back to nature" ideas: not only the cultivation of the land but the building of houses and cities too was seen as an important part of human destiny. It has sometimes been pointed out that the Bible story begins with a garden and ends with a city. When civilized land returns to the wild it is usually seen as a result of something human beings have done wrong. Among the prophecies of judgment are pictures of vineyards becoming rough heath covered in briers and thorns (Is 7:23-25). The downfall of the glorious city of Babylon is described in a picture of wild animals prowling in the ruins of its buildings (Is 13:19-22). Conversely, the renewal of the people is accompanied by renewed fruitfulness. Creation itself shares in the people's joy: "The wilderness and the dry land shall be glad, the desert shall rejoice and blossom" (Is 35:1-2). This theme is taken up in the New Testament, when Paul looks to the day when "the creation itself will be set free from its bondage to decay and will obtain the freedom of the glory of the children of God" (Rom 8:21).

We today may express things differently. Jeremiah's nightmare vision strongly suggests the ecological disaster we fear for the planet today, or the effects of nuclear war, but we part company with him when he sees cities laid in ruins "before the LORD, before his fierce anger". We can see how human greed and carelessness can devastate the earth. We acknowledge too that there are disasters such as earthquakes that have nothing to do with human causes, but we see them as accidental, part of the inevitable conditions we live with on this planet. We find it much harder than Jeremiah did to believe that God in his anger deliberately causes these things to happen. Here again we are faced with the fact that the Bible is culturally alien to us and yet at the same time often shockingly relevant. Jeremiah and the other prophets described things in the language of their religion and world view, but the fundamental principle is the same. What they were saying was that the greed and false values of human beings can have disastrous effects on the environment, but when human beings live justly there is a peace, a "rightness" that overflows into the natural order itself.

Concern for the environment is now, thankfully, a major issue among many Christians. Some have been slow to catch on to it. Shamefully, there have been conservative Christians who dismissed this concern for the very reason that it was associated with "new age". However, the theme of God as Creator and the relationship between humanity and the environment is an important one throughout the Bible. The creation story in the first chapter of Genesis, with its culmination in the creation of human beings to have "dominion", has often been misunderstood. It has been interpreted as giving human beings the right to do whatever they like to the planet, to simply exploit it for their own enrichment and comfort. But this is not a necessary meaning of the saying. "Dominion" can mean a power that is meant to be exercised responsibly. Something of this meaning comes out in the other creation story, where Adam is placed in the Garden of Eden "to till it and keep it" (Gen 2:15). The way to honour the earth is not to leave it to itself but to cultivate and steward it responsibly. The true "dominion" is what we see practised in the efforts being made to restore damaged environments or to save endangered species. In this, we human beings are using our intelligence and technology to do for other species what they are not able to do for themselves.

We still have our nightmares and our dreams. Perhaps today the nightmares tend to prevail, with fears of ecological disaster, climate change, the destruction of biodiversity, and so on. At the same time we look for reasons to be hopeful. Some do this by trying to deny the whole idea of climate change. Others are confident that scientific research will find a way to avert the worst effects. Many probably take refuge in the idea that humanity, faced with a crisis, will as usual come to its senses just in time. This last view is probably the nearest to the biblical one: the prophecies of disaster and destruction may sound like straightforward predictions, but they were almost always meant as warnings. The Book of Jonah tells how God sent Jonah to warn the people of Nineveh that their city would be destroyed in forty days. However, the people repented of their wickedness and humbled themselves before God, and so God "changed his mind" about his threat (Jon 3:10). The King James Version uses the word "repented", a difficult idea perhaps from a philosophical point of view, but very expressive of the dynamic of Israel's sense of relationship with a living God. The threat of judgment was never final and irrevocable: it was a wake-up call.

In modern times there have also been much more positive

dreams. All kinds of diseases have been eliminated. Medical scientists talk of finding a cure for the aging process and of babies born today possibly living well beyond a century. There are ways of solving the problem of world hunger if only the political will is there. Fifty years ago, John F Kennedy said:

> "Never before has man had such capacity to control his own environment, to end thirst and hunger, to conquer poverty and disease, to banish illiteracy and massive human misery. We have the power to make this the best generation of mankind in the history of the world or to make it the last."[1]

That did not turn out to be literally true. Visionaries are often right in their ultimate vision but usually inaccurate in their timing. However, it is certainly true today that the world has immense possibilities for progress in human wellbeing alongside equally immense possibilities of disaster.

Apocalypse

Some of the writers who contributed to the Bible took these cosmic visions of doom and glory a step further, and produced a type of literature that scholars refer to as "apocalyptic". It appears especially in parts of the Book of Daniel and in the Book of Revelation. These are the tip of the iceberg of a vast literature that appeared in the few centuries before and after the time of Jesus. "Apocalypse" is the Greek equivalent of the Latin "revelation": both mean "unveiling". In early Christian times there were many Apocalypses stemming from both the Jewish and the Christian communities. Most of the Jewish ones were too late to be considered as part of the canon of Jewish scripture. It is significant that the Book of Daniel, which is included among the prophets in the Christian Old Testament, is not so in the Jewish Bible, but appears in the miscellaneous writings towards the end. There were numerous Christian apocalypses, but only one, the

"Revelation of St John the Divine", ultimately found a place in the New Testament, and even that one was one of the last books to be fully accepted by the ancient church and the first to be questioned in modern times: Luther's Bible includes it with a few others as a kind of appendix.

There are other, briefer, pieces of apocalypse in the Bible. The last chapter of Zechariah is one, as is the discourse of Jesus in the Gospels (Matt 24; Mark 13; Luke 21), in which the prediction of the destruction of the Temple (which happened in 70 CE) seems to be merged with the coming of the Son of Man and the final judgment. It is hard to tell how much of this was said by Jesus and how much was embellished after the events of 70 CE, nor can we know exactly what Jesus meant by these things if he did say them.

The chief characteristic of apocalyptic writing is that it claims to "unveil" the secrets of God's purpose for the future of the whole world. It often speaks in code language, because it was written at a time when forces hostile to Judaism or Christianity were very powerful, and it was dangerous to speak directly. In the Book of Revelation, for instance, the various ferocious beasts are rulers, probably Roman emperors, and the whore who sits on seven hills, drunk with the blood of the saints (Rev 17), is Rome, also called (in chapter 18) Babylon, the name of the chief oppressor of the Jews in earlier times.

These apocalyptic books are a happy hunting ground for people who believe the Bible forecasts the future course of world history. Somehow, their calculations always lead to the conclusion that the events forecast are happening in the period in which they themselves are living! However, the most helpful way to understand apocalyptic writing is to see in it coded references to the writer's own time. The Book of Daniel, for instance, was almost certainly produced in its present form in the second century BCE, when Jerusalem and the Jewish way of life were under serious threat from the Syrian regime. The "abomination that desolates" (Dan 9:28; 12:11), known more familiarly as "the abomination of desolation" (Matt 24:15; Mark 13:14, AV) was the setting up of an image of the Greek God Zeus in the Temple in Jerusalem. Daniel had a vision of four great beasts coming up out of the sea, one like a lion, one like a bear, one like a leopard, and then one so horrible and strong that it was not like any other animal. These were probably symbols of four great empires that had oppressed the Jews – the Babylonians, the Medes, the Persians and the Syrian kings. Then there is a judgment scene in Heaven, and the appearance of "one like a son of man" who was given an everlasting dominion over the nations (Dan 7:13). This one represents "the people of the holy ones of the Most High" (v27), which presumably means the true worshippers of God who will ultimately rule the world, and whose rule will be a truly human one.

A New World Now

By the time of Jesus the prophetic and apocalyptic vision had mostly crystallized into the idea of the kingdom of God. The phrase "kingdom of heaven" is probably a synonym devised out of the reverence that made Jewish people reluctant to talk too much about God. It does not indicate a kingdom up in the sky: it means something more like the "kingship" or "rule" of God, and reflects the hope that a day was coming when that rule would become manifest in the world. In the words of the Lord's Prayer: "thy kingdom come, thy will be done on earth as it is in heaven".

This kingdom was associated with the restoration of the kingship of David, who had been promised an eternal dynasty. In the minds of many people, it would be brought about by a "Son of David", a new Messiah ("anointed one").

According to the Gospels Jesus talked a lot about this Kingdom of Heaven. Many of his parables begin with "the kingdom of heaven is like...". Sometimes the image is of judgment, but sometimes too it is of a transformation of the world. There is an ambiguity about it: sometimes it seems to be something that is to happen in the future, at a date that no-one knows, but at other times it seems to be a present reality, or at least a present possibility. Jesus sometimes invited people to live in the Kingdom of Heaven here and now by embracing its ways and values.

An essential part of the hope for Israel was the gathering in of all Israelites from the various places to which they had been exiled. Jesus seems to have taken this in a new way, as not just a gathering of faithful Jewish people scattered around the nations, but the integration of the whole nation, including those who were not devout and faithful: the tax collectors, the people living a life inconsistent with the religious laws, all who were despised and outcast by the more religious. When the Pharisees criticized the way he mingled with all manner of people, he said, "I have come to call not the righteous but sinners" (Mark 2:17). When Zacchaeus the dishonest and unpopular tax collector had a complete change of heart as a result of Jesus visiting his home, Jesus said of him, "he too is a son of Abraham" (Luke 19:9). In other words Zacchaeus, in spite of his uncleanness in the sight of orthodox Jews, and even of the way he was betraying his people by profiting from his co-operation with the Romans, was in the eyes of Jesus still one of the family, one needing to be "gathered in".

Jesus seems also to have been looking for the purifying of the Jewish nation. He called upon them to live consistently with their nature as a holy people, to worship God before all other things and not to be drawn into the worship of money, power and prestige. The fact of his choosing twelve apostles and talking of them judging the twelve tribes of Israel (Luke 22:30) is probably symbolic of his vision of a new, reformed people of God.

It is not clear how far Jesus himself thought beyond the confines of the Jewish people. They were obviously the main focus of his vision. Matthew says that when he sent out his disciples on a preaching mission he specifically told them not to go to Gentiles or Samaritans, but to concentrate on "the lost sheep of the house of Israel" (Matt 10:5-6). This is a saying that we can fairly confidently assume to come from Jesus himself rather than from later tradition or the writer of the Gospel: a command like this would not sit comfortably with the attitude of Christians of a later generation. On the other hand, when we read in John's Gospel that he said, "I have other sheep that do not belong to this fold. I must bring them also" (John 10:16), and when in his parting words to the disciples he sends them out to the whole world (Matt 28:19; Acts 1:8), we have to bear in mind the possibility that these are interpretations of Jesus read back from the point of view of the later history of the church. Nevertheless, there are strong hints that Jesus himself had a wider vision. For example, there is the story of his encounter with the Roman centurion, when he said he had not seen such faith as this in Israel, and prophesied: "many will come from east and west and will eat with Abraham and Isaac and Jacob in the kingdom of heaven" (Matt 8:10-11). There was also his visit to the synagogue in Nazareth when he pointed out that sometimes foreigners received blessings the Jews themselves were not ready to receive (Luke 4:25-27). Whether by the direct teaching of Jesus or by the early Christians' reflection on him, Christianity very quickly developed the vision of a new world which believers were called to declare, and at the same time to anticipate by their way of life.

Community with Diversity

The biblical dream of a new world is very much bound up with peace. The question is: what kind of peace? Often it is seen simply as the absence of opposition to the God the writer believes in. This is the vision of Isaiah: the reason why the nations will "beat their swords into ploughshares, and their spears into pruning hooks" is that they will all be coming to the Temple in Jerusalem to learn the ways of the God of Israel (Is 2:2-4). In the New Testament, Jesus sends his followers to "make disciples of all nations... teaching them to obey everything that I have commanded you" (Matt 28:19-20). The hymn of praise in Paul's Letter to the Philippians says that Jesus has been exalted above all others so that "at the name of Jesus every knee should bow" (Phil 2:10, AV). This was the vision behind the missionary movement of the nineteenth century and the early part of the twentieth, when European Christians held up the ideal of a peaceful world brought about by the irresistible spread of Christianity.

Today we have had to come to terms with a world in which there are different religions, often practised by people living alongside each other as neighbours. At a time when the European nations, especially Great Britain, were the most powerful in the world and claimed the right to rule the rest of it, it was assumed that Christianity and civilization were virtually synonymous. Britain and the other Christian nations not only colonized other parts of the world but sent missionaries to evangelize them too. The non-Christian faiths (with the exception of Judaism) were associated with less "civilized" people, and thought to have had their day. A small minority of Christian missionaries and of colonial administrators held the other religions in great respect and took an interest in learning about them, but the attitude of most was, at best, one of patron-ising toleration.

Today, no one religion can regard itself as politically or socially privileged. Legislation in most Western countries requires that people be free to practise their faith, and makes it a criminal offence to discriminate against people or abuse them on the ground of their religion. Religious education in schools (compulsory in the United Kingdom and some other countries) is no longer instruction in Christianity but the study of the whole range of religious traditions.

Certain practical tensions arise when the liberal, egalitarian principles of secular society clash with traditions that seem illiberal but are part of sacred tradition. Should Muslim women, for instance, be allowed to appear in public with their faces covered? How far should arranged or enforced marriages be tolerated in Western society? Are ritual ways of slaughtering animals unnecessarily cruel, and if so should they be allowed? Has any church or religious organization the right to discriminate against women? Does the upholding of civil rights mean that people should be compelled, whatever their religious scruples, to give hospitality and employment to practising homosexuals? How strongly should adherents of one religion be allowed to voice in public their opposition to the beliefs of another? Issues like this remind us that religious differences are real, and that treating all religions equally is not as simple as it may seem at first sight. We have to recognize that realistic peace can only be achieved if we face up to the reality of difference.

Quite apart from the practical issues, the existence of different religions is a theological problem for many believers. Most Christians will never compromise their belief that Jesus Christ is the only-begotten Son of God and that the only way to salvation is to believe in his atoning death and Resurrection. For Muslims, it is blasphemy to say that God has a son, and the only way to be fully acceptable in the sight of God is to believe that Mohammed is the final prophet and that the Qur'an is the perfect revealed Word of God. For people of other religions, such as Hindus, Buddhists and Sikhs, there are many ways to spiritual enlightenment, and so all religions can be respected and perhaps even regarded as equal. Most Christians and Muslims, however, insist that there is only one way, and disagree fundamentally as to which way that is.

On this major issue of our time the Bible at first sight seems to be firmly on the side of dogmatism and exclusiveness. The

Hebrew scriptures constantly condemn the worship of any God but the God of Israel, and forbid the making of any image of God. They also, as we have seen, include extremely harsh passages commanding the Israelites to slaughter all idol-worshippers without mercy. But much of the Christian rejection of other religions comes from the New Testament. Jesus is represented as saying. "I am the Way, the Truth and the Life. No one comes to the Father except through me" (John 14:6), and one of his early disciples as saying, "there is no other name under heaven given among mortals by which we must be saved" (Acts 4:12). Here, however, we need to beware of interpreting the Bible within the framework of traditional Christian dogma and assuming that it means what we have been taught it means. We have to look at the context of these sayings and ask who said them and why.

These sayings were coined in the heat of controversy between the early Christians and their Jewish compatriots. From the point of view of the Christians, the Jewish leaders of that time had disqualified themselves from the favour of God by condemning Jesus and persecuting his followers. The rigidity of their religious traditions had blinded them to the presence of God among them in Jesus. The salvation for which the Jews had waited and prayed for centuries was now right under their noses, and they had rejected it. Peter was telling them that there was no other way of salvation. Having rejected Jesus, what other Saviour could they expect? The saying in John's Gospel about Jesus being the only way comes from a time when the Christian church had grown so far away from its Jewish origin that "the Jews" were now seen as the opposition.

The controversy, however, was between the Christians and the Jewish community at a time when the condemnation and crucifixion of Jesus was still very recent. We need not interpret these sayings as referring to Hindus or Buddhists who, though perhaps not completely unknown, were not in practice part of the world in which Christianity began. They could not have referred to the Muslim community, which was not yet in existence. Nor, for that matter, should they be applied to Jews of today who are the heirs to two thousand more years of history and who have every reason to be sceptical about Jesus in the light of the way they have been treated by those who claim to represent him.

We have to remember too that the Bible itself is a mixed collection of writings by many different people in different times and circumstances. Once we release it from the dead hand of fixed doctrines, we discover that it is a multi-cultural and even in some ways multi-faith set of writings. The Hebrew scriptures are not purely Hebrew in their culture. Ancient Israelite culture was already a mixture of influences from Egypt, Mesopotamia and other places. In spite of the thundering of the prophets, we have to acknowledge that many characteristics of Israel's beliefs and worship probably came from the Canaanite environment. During and after the Exile, the Jews absorbed ideas from Babylon and Persia. One of these was probably the belief in life after death which the Sadducees, being conservative, refused to accept.

After the conquests of Alexander in the late fourth century BCE the whole of the Middle East came under the influence of Greek culture. The Hebrew scriptures were translated into Greek, and by the time the New Testament came to be written Greek was the natural language of international communication in the eastern Mediterranean region and possibly further west as well – even Paul's Letter to the Romans was written in Greek. Jews were beginning to interpret the scriptures in ways influenced by Greek philosophy, and we only have to look at the first chapter of John's Gospel to see that Greek concepts were beginning to have a major influence on Christian thinking. This influence was greatly strengthened as Christianity moved westward. The major accepted doctrines of the Christian faith like the Incarnation and the Trinity are expressed in the language of Greek philosophy, and yet the majority of Christians have quite easily read them back into the Bible and seen no inconsistency.

In many ways the Bible itself is a blend of different cultures and philosophies, a multi-cultural literature which, if we read it imaginatively, can actually help us to recognize the value of different expressions of faith.

This mixture of cultures was present within the early Christian church. Christianity began as a movement among Jewish people, and its message that Jesus was the promised Messiah seemed at first to be relevant only to Jews. However, at quite an early stage it began to break out of the boundaries. The Christian community in the great cosmopolitan city of Antioch seems to have led the way in this, becoming a rich mixture of Jews and Gentiles. One of the major issues that exercised the Christian church at that time was whether Gentiles could be accepted as part of the church without first becoming Jews. It seems that a council held in Jerusalem (Acts 15) decided that the church would not impose Jewish laws and customs on Gentile converts but would be content that they show some minimal respect for Jewish traditions. However, this remained a burning issue for some time. The question of how far the Jewish laws should be observed was obviously an ongoing problem in the early church.

Paul was the most prominent advocate of the principle that the message of Christ was for all nations and that in Christ a new community was being created in which the old barriers were broken down, a community in which Jews could belong as Jews and Gentiles as Gentiles. His burning conviction about this made him very angry with those who tried to impose Jewish restrictions on Gentile believers. This shows itself in several places in his letters, but nowhere more than in his Letter to the Galatians, where he asserts (Gal 1:8-9) that anyone who preaches a gospel different from the one he preached should be cursed, and that this should apply even to himself if he should ever preach anything different!

Yet, with all this burning conviction, Paul took great pains to set out guidelines for compromise and mutual respect. He reminded both sides, the strict people who judged others and the "liberals" who mocked other people's scruples, that the heart of the gospel they all believed in was love. If people are seeking to serve God according to their own conscience, we have no more right to pass judgment on them than we have to discipline someone else's servant (Rom 14:4). Our aim should be to uphold one another, and it is better to keep one's convictions to oneself than to give needless offence to others (Rom 14:20-22). Evidently for Paul, as for many of us today, convictions are important, but living with other people is important too, and the tension between these two principles can often lead us onto a complex and tricky path.

Another issue that troubled some of the early Gentile Christians was that of meat that had been "offered to idols". Animal sacrifice was virtually universal in the culture of the Greco-Roman world, and the carcasses, if they had not been burned, were disposed of in different ways. Sometimes the meat was eaten by the congregation as part of the ceremony of sacrifice, or it was food for the priests and temple workers. Sometimes, however, it ended up in the meat market, and for Christians this presented a problem. By eating meat that had been sacrificed to a false god, were they condoning idolatrous religion, or even perhaps participating in an idolatrous communion? Paul, in his first Letter to the Corinthians, firmly warns them against taking part in idolatrous religious feasts. These, he says, are totally incompatible with the fact that they share in the Christian Eucharist: "You cannot drink the cup of the Lord and the cup of demons. You cannot partake of the table of the Lord and the table of demons". At the same time, he does not encourage them to ask questions about meat they buy in the market, or about meat that is offered to them when they are guests in someone else's home. Only if they are specifically told it has been offered in sacrifice should they refuse it, and that more for the sake of the other person's conscience than their own (1 Cor 10:14-32).

And so the early Christian church was already an experiment in multiculturalism. The challenges facing us today were present then. The New Testament is highly relevant to us in this regard, but of course we do not need to take it rigidly as a model. We can enter into the debate and ask further, still more challenging, questions. Has the time now come to welcome yet another new vision of "God's people" in which people of different faiths can be themselves and still belong? What compromises can we find acceptable to this end, and are there principles on which we have to dig in our heels and refuse to be moved?

What is the fundamental insight of Christianity that is not negotiable? Many of us would say that it is the conception of God in terms of absolute love rather than absolute power, or the power of love rather than the power of compulsion. Others might express it in different ways but, just like the situation faced by the early church reflected in the New Testament, the world we live in today faces us with a challenge to deep, radical thinking if religion is to make a significant contribution to peace rather than division.

Notes

1. Address before the 18th General Assembly of the United Nations, September 20th, 1963

12

The Elusive Jesus

"No one knows the Son except the Father"
(Matt 11:27)

The central figure of the New Testament, and for Christians the centre of the whole Bible, is Jesus. All the New Testament writers believed that he was in some way the ultimate revelation of God. They call him "the Son of God" (Mark 1:1; Luke 1:35; Rom 1:4; 8:3; Heb 1:2 etc.). John's Gospel calls him the "only" Son of God: the King James Bible translates it more literally as "only begotten" (John 1:18; 3:16). John also says that in him the eternal Word "became flesh" (John 1:14). The Letter to the Colossians calls him "the image of the invisible God" in whom "all the fullness of God was pleased to dwell" (Col 1:15.19). The Letter to the Hebrews says he is "the reflection of God's glory and the exact imprint of God's very being" (Heb 1:3).

Different Stories

But who is this Jesus, and what do we know of him? One of the first things we have to come to terms with is that the New Testament gives us the story of Jesus in four different versions. Many of the differences are small, a matter of wording or of slightly different interpretation. Some of them, however, are major contradictions, and this is particularly true of the central stories: his birth, his death, and his Resurrection.

The traditional nativity plays with the shepherds and the "three kings" gathered in the stable have blinded us to the fact that the Gospels of Matthew and Luke tell two quite different stories about the birth of Jesus which cannot both be historically true. Matthew says that Jesus was born in Bethlehem, and visited by "wise men" from the East who had seen his star rise. King Herod wanted to destroy this potential king of the Jews, so he ordered the killing of all the boys in the region of Bethlehem who were under two years old. This implies that the visit of the wise men took place at least some months after the birth of Jesus. Meanwhile Joseph and Mary, having been warned in a dream, had escaped with Jesus to Egypt. They returned from there some considerable time later, after Herod had died, but thinking that Bethlehem was still not a safe place for them they went further north into Galilee and settled in "a town called Nazareth".

According to Luke's story, however, Nazareth was already their home: it was to Nazareth that the angel Gabriel came to tell Mary about the child she was going to bear (Luke 1:26). She and Joseph had to go to Bethlehem because of a census called by the Roman Emperor. They were temporary visitors there who could not even find proper shelter for the birth of the child. They stayed there just long enough to attend the Temple in Jerusalem for the ceremony of purification and presentation. This, according to the ritual instructions (Lev 12), would have been about a month after the birth. Then, says Luke: "When they had finished everything required by the law of the Lord, they returned to Galilee, to their own town of Nazareth" (Luke 2:39).

Turning to the Gospels of Mark and John, we find no account of the birth of Jesus at all. To Mark, it was evidently not an essential part of the story. John talks of the Word becoming flesh (John 1:14), but he too starts the story of Jesus with his first public appearance as an adult.

When we come to the account of the trial and death of Jesus, we find that Matthew, Mark and Luke say that on the evening before his death Jesus ate the Passover meal with his disciples (Matt 26:17; Mark 14:12; Luke 22:7-8). However, John's account is different. It says that they had a meal together the night before his death, but does not mention that it was the Passover meal. In the account of the trial the next morning, it says that when the

Jewish leaders brought Jesus to Pilate the Roman governor, they would not go into Pilate's headquarters for fear of defiling themselves and being unable to eat the Passover (John 18:28). Later it says three times that the day of the crucifixion was "the day of preparation" for the Passover (John 19:14.31.42). And so it seems the Gospels disagree as to whether Jesus died on the Passover day or the next day.

The stories of the Resurrection are equally confusing. All four Gospels tell us of the tomb being found empty on the morning of the first day of the week, but they differ in detail as to who went to the tomb and what they saw. Was it two women, three, or more? Or was it just Mary Magdalene? And what did they see: a young man, an angel, two men or two angels? On the other hand Paul, in the earliest written account we have of the Resurrection, repeats the story as it was given to him, but does not mention the women or the empty tomb at all. (Compare Matt 28:1-10; Mark 16:1-8; Luke 24:1-12; John 20:1-18; 1 Cor 15:3-7).

These differences in detail can be partly explained (but surely only partly) by the fact that different people inevitably remember the same event in different ways, and that perhaps even at the time the whole thing was so mysterious and overwhelming that everyone was confused as to what was happening. However, there is a much more serious discrepancy. In Luke all the appearances of the risen Jesus take place in or near Jerusalem during a period of forty days. In Matthew the only time the disciples see him is on a mountain in Galilee. John's Gospel includes appearances both in Jerusalem and in Galilee, but this does not help us to get around the inconsistency between Matthew and Luke. According to Luke, Jesus actually told the disciples to stay in Jerusalem until they had received the power of the Holy Spirit – an event that happened on the day of Pentecost, seven weeks after the Resurrection. But according to Matthew and Mark the disciples were expressly told to go to meet him in Galilee. Both Matthew and Luke (in Acts 1) bring the story of Jesus to a climax with his parting command to his disciples to spread the message throughout the world, but where did this happen? Luke says it happened on the Mount of Olives outside Jerusalem, but according to Matthew it was on a mountain in Galilee. And so, both on the death and the Resurrection of Jesus, the Gospels tell different and incompatible stories.

Many people have tried to "harmonize" the Gospels. It was attempted as early as about 160 CE by a scholar called Tatian who produced the *Diatessaron* ("through four"), a continuous narrative of the life of Jesus based on the four Gospels. These "harmonies", in trying to show that all the Gospel accounts are historically true, usually end up as a very complicated story that is hard to believe. They also leave unanswered the question of why some of the Gospel writers were so ignorant of some of the major events. For instance, the raising of Lazarus (John 11), who had been dead for four days, would surely have been a sensation not easily forgotten, yet Matthew, Mark and Luke do not mention it. Matthew tells how, at the moment Jesus died, dead people came out of their tombs, walked around in Jerusalem and "appeared to many" (Matt 27:52-53). The other Gospels seem totally ignorant of this. This surely raises questions about whether these things happened in just the way they are described.

The Meaning of the Story

With the story of Jesus, as with the Israelite histories, we are in the realm of interpreted history or, looking at it from the other direction, a message backed up by stories. The Gospels were all written some decades after the events. Stories of Jesus had been circulating all that time, but not in any particular order. The early followers of Jesus were convinced that he was returning to establish his kingdom in the very near future, and so they had no incentive to preserve an ordered account of his whole life. It was the Gospel writers who built up an ordered account from the various stories they had, and so it is hardly surprising that the order is different in different gospels, or that stories appear in different versions. They were creatively and imaginatively weaving the little stories together to make a big story with a big message.

The Gospels were not meant to be history for the sake of history. Each one is a kind of sermon. It draws on handed down memories of Jesus and tells its own story according to the insights of the final author or compiler. What we have is a picture of Jesus reflected through his influence on different people. Like all the Bible stories, the stories of Jesus came out of people's attempts to understand the meaning of what had happened to them. The most relevant question to ask of each Gospel writer is not "what really happened?" but "what does Jesus mean to *you*?" The question, of course, is not quite as personal as that, because the Gospels grew out of the traditions of Christian communities. The people responsible for their final form were not so much individual authors as compilers and editors. We cannot say how much of their personal stamp is on the story they tell: it is an account of what Jesus meant to the community in which that particular Gospel was formed.

The first disciples had followed Jesus because he seemed to be a great prophet, talking of the imminent kingdom of God. They came to believe he was the Messiah, the one sent by God to restore Israel to its proper glory. But then he had been arrested, condemned and executed as a criminal. This could have been the end of all their hopes, but some of them had experiences that convinced them that he was alive again and sharing in the power and authority of God. The horror of his death and the growing conviction of his indestructible life meant that they had to make sense of the whole story in the light of their faith in God. How could the crucifixion be within God's purpose for the Messiah?

For Saul of Tarsus, later to be called Paul, there was a different challenge. He was not one of those who had known Jesus "in the flesh", been devastated by his death, and needed to make sense of it at the time. What he had to come to terms with was a remarkable life-changing experience that happened later. His first reaction to Jesus was outrage at the way people were talking of this crucified criminal as the Messiah. It threatened the system of beliefs and practices around which his life revolved. He felt it his duty to stamp out this new disruptive and blasphemous movement. Then, on the way to Damascus to round up and arrest the followers of Jesus there, he had a dramatic conversion which resulted in his becoming one of the most prominent preachers of the new way. The unusual nature of his conversion gave him a way of looking at Jesus that was different.

First, he was acutely aware of having been forgiven. Secondly, the particular Christian community he was drawn into was the one at Antioch, one of the main cities of the Roman Empire. In that cosmopolitan city the Christian community was cosmopolitan too. Paul discovered there a deep fellowship that broke down all the barriers of ethnicity and social class. Jews and Gentiles were eating together. Slaves and slave owners were relating to each other like brothers and sisters. This brought home to him what a new, transforming power had been let loose in the world through Jesus, and challenged him to explore what it all meant. He began to see the relevance of the Christian message not just for Jews who had been taught to expect the Messiah, but for the whole world. He began to formulate his vision of a new human unity forged by the death of Jesus on the cross. The Jewish religious law that had condemned Jesus had been exposed in its ineffectiveness, and the shedding of the blood of Jesus had become the sacrifice to atone for the sins of both Jews and Gentiles on equal terms: "All have sinned and fall short of the glory of God; they are now justified by his grace as a gift, through the redemption that is in Christ Jesus..." (Rom 3:23).

The story by which Paul made sense of Jesus was in a way

truncated and minimal. He did not have much to say about the life and teaching of Jesus. For him, the good news was all summed up in his death and Resurrection. The Gospels tell the rest of the story, each looking for its meaning in its own distinctive way.

The writer (or compiler) of Matthew's Gospel sees Jesus as the fulfilment of the Jewish hope and its opening up to the whole world. He begins the story with a genealogy showing how Jesus was descended from Abraham, to whom God had promised a great nation, and from David, who had been promised an eternal dynasty. He emphasizes the way in which Jesus fulfilled the prophecies of the scriptures. He gives us a solid body of the teaching of Jesus delivered on a mountain, just as Moses brought the Law of God down from Mount Sinai. The early life of Jesus has already echoed that of Moses: both were rescued from a massacre of baby boys ordered by a king. Matthew records Jesus as saying: "Do not think that I have come to abolish the law or the prophets; I have come not to abolish but to fulfil." (Matt 5:17)

At the same time, the global dimension of the meaning of Jesus is shown in the story of astrologers from the East coming with gifts for the baby Jesus, recognizing that he had come into the world for them too (Matt 2:1-12). It is shown again by the parable of the sheep and the goats, in which when the Son of Man comes in his glory "all the nations will be gathered before him", and they will be judged not by their ethnicity or their doctrines, but by how they have treated the least of the members of his family, whether they recognized him in them or not (Matt 25:31-46). Finally it is shown in the farewell words of Jesus to his disciples: "All authority in heaven and on earth has been given to me. Go therefore and make disciples of all nations" (Matt 28:18-19).

Mark's Gospel is shorter. It omits any reference to the birth or childhood of Jesus. The "beginning of the good news of Jesus Christ" for Mark is the appearance of John the Baptist as a herald in the desert, his baptizing of Jesus, and the voice from Heaven declaring Jesus to be the Beloved Son of God. Things move quite quickly: one of Mark's favourite words is "immediately". Jesus is presented as a miracle worker who draws ever more astonished response from people who see what is happening. However, he himself tends to draw back from this recognition. When the crowd comes looking for him as a healer, he withdraws to a solitary place to pray, and then moves on (Mark 1:35-39). Sometimes, after healing someone, he tells them not to tell anyone (Mark 1:43-44; 5:43; 7:36). He seems not to want recognition of his status as the Son of God (Mark 3:11-12). According to Mark, when Peter declared "You are the Messiah", Jesus, as in Matthew's telling of the story, ordered them not to tell anyone, but did not react with the joy and enthusiasm described by Matthew (compare Mark 8:29-30 with Matt 16:20). Then, as the account approaches his trial and death, there is a distinct change of tone. Jesus has suddenly become more like a victim, suffering, mocked and helpless. As in Matthew, his last words on the cross are: "My God, my God, why have you forsaken me?" (Mark 15:34; Matt 27:46).

However, unlike in Matthew, there are no spectacular accompaniments to his death other than the tearing of the curtain in the Temple. There is no earthquake and no rising of bodies from the graves. The Resurrection too is much more low-key. If we accept the end of Mark's Gospel given by the most reliable ancient manuscripts, the story ends with the women, having been told that Jesus is alive but not having seen him, running away from the tomb in "terror and amazement" and being afraid to say anything to anyone. And so Mark's presentation of the story of Jesus is a kind of whirlwind career with a sudden end that leaves questions hanging in the air. There may even be an intended irony in the fact that the people Jesus had healed were told not to talk about it and did, while the first witnesses of the Resurrection were told to pass on the news and did not.

Luke lays great emphasis on the inclusive friendship and compassion of Jesus and his relationships with the outcasts of society. This is expressed in a number of stories that are not found in the other Gospels. One particularly provocative one is the story (Luke 7:36-50) of how, while Jesus was dining at the home of a Pharisee, a notorious woman of the town came in, wept over his feet, dried them with her hair and spread ointment on them, and how Jesus set her up as an example to the righteous Pharisee of how to show love! It is only Luke who tells the story of the peaceable way in which Jesus took rejection by a Samaritan village (Luke 9:51-56), and of the conversion of Zacchaeus the tax-collector when Jesus chose to visit his home (Luke 19:1-10). It is to Luke that we owe some of the most popular and striking parables like the Good Samaritan (Luke 10:25-37) and the Prodigal Son (Luke 15:11-32).

Luke, more than the others, sees the coming of Jesus in radical social terms, as the promise of a change in society. He depicts his mother Mary singing of bringing down the powerful from their thrones and lifting up the lowly, of filling the hungry with good things and sending the rich away empty (1:52-53). It is in Luke's Gospel that we are told that the baby Jesus was laid in a manger because there was no room at the inn, and that his birth was announced to shepherds on the night watch (2:7-20). Luke adds to the account of John the Baptist's preaching a challenge to radical sharing: "Whoever has two coats must share with anyone who has none..." (3:11). He tells of Jesus in the synagogue at Nazareth using a passage from the Book of Isaiah as the "manifesto" of his own mission "to bring good news to the poor... to proclaim release to the captives... to let the oppressed go free." (Luke 4:18).

However, it is also interesting to note what is missing in Luke's Gospel. There is nothing of the significance that Paul attaches to the death of Jesus. Luke omits the saying about the Son of Man giving his life as a ransom (Matt 20:28; Mark 10:45).

His view of the death of Jesus seems to be simply that it was the necessary prelude to his entering into his glory, as foretold in the scriptures (Luke 24:26,46).

Forgiveness is an important theme in Luke's understanding of Jesus, both in the Gospel and in its sequel, the Acts of the Apostles. At the end of the Gospel Jesus says that the climax of the whole story of his death and Resurrection is that "repentance and forgiveness of sins is to be proclaimed in his name to all nations." (Luke 24:47). Peter, on the day of Pentecost, asserts that this Jesus "whom you crucified" is the Lord and Messiah, calls upon the people to repent and be baptized to identify themselves with him, and promises that they will receive forgiveness and the gift of the Holy Spirit (Acts 2:36-38). Later Luke tells how Paul, speaking in a synagogue, told the Jews there that Jesus had risen from the dead and that everyone who believes in him will be set free from their sins (Acts 13:39).

For Luke, this forgiveness is not linked to any idea of the death of Jesus being an atoning sacrifice for sin. He tells how Jesus prayed on the cross: "Father, forgive them, for they know not what they do." (Luke 23:14). This is a saying that is not present in all manuscripts, but matches well with the attitude and message of Luke. In any case, Luke is the only one who tells how one of the criminals being crucified with Jesus said, "Jesus, remember me when you come into your kingdom", and Jesus answered, "Truly I tell you, today you will be with me in Paradise" (Luke 23:39-43). According to Luke Jesus, with almost his last breath, was still declaring forgiveness to sinners. The "Father, forgive them" saying seems to be taken up again in what Peter says to the people after the healing of the lame man at the Temple gate: "And now, friends, I know that you acted in ignorance... repent therefore , and turn to God so that your sins may be wiped out" (Acts 3:17-19).

Luke, then, makes sense of the story of Jesus by seeing it as foretold in the Hebrew scriptures, and seeing him as practising a ministry of forgiveness to sinners and openness to all people during his earthly life and then, having suffered and risen from the dead, opening up the message of judgment and forgiveness to the whole world.

The writer of John's Gospel sees Jesus in a way quite different from the others. He begins with the cosmic dimension, seeing him as the incarnation of the divine Word that was part of God from eternity, the light that enlightens all humanity. At the same time, he sees Jesus as the Lamb of God who is sacrificed to atone for the sins of the world. Unlike Luke, who pictures Jesus sitting in Heaven until the time comes for him to return and judge the world, John sees the living presence of Jesus in the hearts, lives and actions of those who love him. There is a mystical union of Jesus with God and with all who believe in him. The focus of hope is not the coming of the reign of God in the future, but the experience of eternal life, the "life more abundant" (John 10:10) here and now.

The New Testament has other interpretations of Jesus too. The Letter to the Hebrews interprets his death in terms of the ceremony of the Day of Atonement: Jesus is the ultimate High Priest of whom the Jewish High Priest was but the foreshadowing. He has offered his own blood to atone for the sins of the whole world, and has opened the way for us into the Holy of Holies, Heaven itself.

The Book of Revelation makes Jesus the centre of a story that is yet to be completed. He is the Alpha and Omega, the beginning and the end, the one who will be victorious in all the sufferings and tribulations that will happen in the world until God brings down from Heaven the New Jerusalem and death and pain will be no more.

It is these differences in the understanding of the meaning of Jesus that lie behind some of the discrepancies in the Gospels. John, for instance, in saying that Jesus was crucified on the morning before the Passover meal, probably intended to show

Jesus, the "Lamb of God" (John 1:29,36) being crucified at the same time as the Passover lambs were being killed in the Temple. The other three Gospel writers perhaps wanted to show that Jesus used the Passover meal, which celebrated the release from slavery in Egypt, as the declaration of a new act of liberation.

The two inconsistent accounts of the Resurrection could well reflect a disagreement about the basis and nature of the church. Perhaps the people among whom Luke's Gospel emerged were particularly keen to show that the Christian mission had its origin with the Apostles in Jerusalem, and was therefore based on apostolic authority (perhaps an early idea of the apostolic succession) while the producers of Matthew's Gospel were more aligned with those who emphasized the priority of the teaching ministry of Jesus in Galilee.

And so the writers of the New Testament, all in their different ways, sought to make sense of Jesus, not just his teaching, but the story of what happened to him and the spiritual experience of his continued living presence, and to make sense of their lives and the world in the light of all this.

The "Jesus of History" and the "Christ of Faith"

Apart from the differing accounts of the birth, death and Resurrection there are innumerable discrepancies in the Gospel accounts of what Jesus did and said. There are also discrepancies between some of the sayings attributed to Jesus on the one hand and, on the other hand, what historians perceive as the setting of Jesus' ministry and his own understanding of himself. For example, the way in which Jesus talked of the imminent Kingdom of Heaven makes it hard to imagine that he meant to found a permanent organization. This means that there is room for doubt on the quoted teachings of Jesus that relate to disciplinary procedures in the church (Matt 18:15-17) and the saying (unique to Matthew) that Peter would be the rock on which Jesus would build his church (Matt 16:18). The reticence Jesus had about being called the Messiah, evident in the first three Gospels, makes it hard to believe that Jesus could really have told a Samaritan woman that he was the Messiah, or uttered some of the other sayings attributed to him in the Gospel of John, like "I am the bread of life", "I am the light of the world", or "before Abraham was, I am" (John 4:26; 6:35; 8:12; 8:58).

For reasons like this, scholars have studied the Gospels very closely with a view to sifting out the genuine sayings and actions of Jesus from the later traditions that developed in the church. Some are very confident that they have a good idea of what Jesus actually said and did and what he did not say or do. Others are less sure. The process that Albert Schweitzer labelled "the quest of the historical Jesus" still goes on. Numerous theories have emerged: Jesus the liberal humanitarian, Jesus the apocalyptic preacher, Jesus the political dissident, Jesus the rebel leader, Jesus the ordinary Jewish rabbi, and so on. It is worth noting that even in the early days of Christianity there were radically different understandings of the kind of person Jesus was and his purpose in the world. Not only are there the differences we have already noted in the four New Testament Gospels, but there are even bigger differences in some of the many Gospels that did not become part of the New Testament. The Gospel of Thomas, while in some ways just as close to the original events as the New Testament Gospels, presents a view of Jesus that tends towards the Gnostic idea of him as one who revealed mysterious truths understood only by the initiated. The Gospel of the Hebrews claims that Jesus was a vegetarian.

No matter how meticulous the scholarship, it is usually impossible to rule out the influence of the scholar's personal feelings about Jesus. The remark made by a Catholic scholar about Harnack's portrayal of Jesus as an ethical humanist is still relevant to many attempts to find the historical Jesus today: "The Christ that Harnack sees... is only the reflection of a Liberal Protestant face, seen at the bottom of a deep well"[1].

The fact is that no matter how much we study we shall never really know exactly what Jesus said and did. The big question is: does it matter? Many theologians stress how what we have in the New Testament and the Christian tradition is not *the Jesus of history* but *the Christ of faith*. In other words, the New Testament writings are shaped by faith in Jesus as the incarnate, crucified and risen Son of God, the Saviour of the world, and the historical details of his life are not an essential part of this. This is to some extent true. Christian faith to this day lives by what Christians believe about the significance of Jesus: his incarnation, death and Resurrection. These beliefs are not affected by the details of his life story. At the same time we surely cannot say that the accuracy of the history does not matter at all. We need some confidence that what we believe is based on someone who really existed and was basically the kind of person the Gospels portray. If this is not the case, then we seem to be creating a Jesus who has no reality outside our imagination.

In fact there emerges from the Gospels a fairly clear picture of a man who excites and inspires many people to this day. Many who are not orthodox Christian believers and have never worried about "the quest of the historical Jesus" are attracted and inspired by the personality and teaching of Jesus. Even if some of the things his followers said about him were inaccurate, exaggerated or imaginary, there is enough there to generate an enduring fascination today even among many people who do not share the Christian faith.

The challenge to live simply, sitting loose to material possessions and taking one day at a time, rings bells for many spiritual seekers today, even though it has rarely been taken seriously by most Christians. In the parable that compares the Kingdom of Heaven to a feast (Luke 14:15-24) the excuses given by the invited guests for not coming were property, work and marriage: the three chief pillars of conventional society. Those who seek a natural communal life unburdened by careers and mortgages find inspiration in the Jesus who is portrayed in the Gospels. The healing activity of Jesus is another aspect that has often bypassed conventional Christianity and resonates with much present-day spirituality. Some of the alternative therapies popular today lay great stress on the power of loving touch, something very close to the way Jesus is portrayed in his healing ministry.

There is in fact a paradox about stories that are not historically true. To take a trivial example: there is an old story of an encounter between Winston Churchill and Bessie Braddock, a Labour Member of Parliament noted for her puritan views and directness, and a "larger than life" character in more ways than one. She is said to have confronted Churchill on one occasion and said, "Winston, you are drunk. You are disgustingly drunk", to which Churchill replied, "My dear Bessie, you are ugly. You are disgustingly ugly. And in the morning I shall be sober". It is disputed whether this exchange actually took place in the way it is described. The story has circulated in many different versions. Sometimes the word used is "fat" rather than "ugly". Sometimes the story features not Bessie Braddock but Lady Nancy Astor, a very different character indeed, but one who is known to have been acquainted with Churchill and to have hated him. In other versions the exchange took place with a woman Churchill passed in the street. With all these uncertainties the fact remains that if you are looking for a story that sums up the character of Winston Churchill, and possibly Bessie Braddock too, you could hardly find a better one. An apocryphal story can often say more about a character than many stories that are strictly factual. It does not necessarily tell us what happened, but it does tell us very clearly that *this was the kind of person about whom a story like that could be told and easily believed.*

In a way the same is true of the stories of Jesus. Whatever the historical accuracy or otherwise of any particular story, we can be reasonably confident that Jesus was the kind of person about whom such a story could be told. With this in mind, we can read the Gospels not in order to establish exactly what happened, but to catch a glimpse of Jesus as a living personality reflected in his effect on the people who knew him and the stories they told about him. There is, in a sense, another Jesus who is neither just the Christ of faith nor the Jesus of history but the Jesus of *story*. This is the Jesus to whom we can confidently say we have direct access in the four New Testament Gospels.

Will We Ever Understand Him?

Whether we take all the sayings and stories of Jesus in the Gospels as factual or whittle them down to a basic core that we feel we can rely on, there is still something very enigmatic and "teasing" about him. He does not seem to have been a systematic theologian with a clear body of teaching. Most of his sayings emerge in dialogue with other people, whether his disciples or his opponents. Like the traditional Jewish rabbis, he seems to have been most at home in challenging and provocative debate.

Sometimes the characters Jesus chooses to tell parables about are unexpected. In one (Matt 20:1-16), he represents God as a wealthy vineyard owner who hires workers at different times of the day but pays those who came in an hour before sunset the same as those who have been working all day. Though this is evidently meant to show God's unconditional generosity, a land owner was not the kind of character the ordinary people listening to Jesus would naturally warm to. Most of them would be more likely to identify with the casual labourers, at the mercy of the land owners as they stood in the market hoping for a chance to earn the rather basic sum of a denarius a day. In another parable (Matt 21:33-44), Jesus seems to liken God to an even less popular character – an absentee landlord who sends his slaves to collect the produce of the vineyard from the tenants. Some of the more affluent Pharisees and Sadducees may have sympathized with the landlord, but the ordinary people listening would have been more likely to take the tenants' side.

The "parable of the talents" (Matt 25:14-30; Luke 19:11-27) is also strange. In this story God is likened to a man who entrusts sums of money to his stewards while he goes away on a journey. On his return, he rewards those who have invested it and made a huge profit, and punishes the one who merely kept it safe, telling him that he could have at least banked it and got interest. Here God seems to be represented as a hard-nosed business man. Moreover, he advocates usury, which was frowned upon by the Jewish scriptures. Another parable (Luke 16:1-9) tells of the antics of a dishonest steward who is about to lose his job but manages to feather his nest right up to the last moment. This man seems to be held up as an example of wisdom.

One suspects that Jesus often spoke tongue-in-cheek and elicited a laugh from his listeners. The parable of the lost sheep (Luke 15:3-7), for instance, starts: "Which one of you, having a hundred sheep and losing one of them, does not leave the ninety-nine in the wilderness and go after the one that is lost until he finds it?" The realistic answer would probably be "no shepherd with any sense would do that!" A sheep is a valuable commodity, but it would be madness to leave ninety-nine sheep unprotected in the wilderness for the sake of one. Perhaps the point Jesus is making is that God is *not* like an earthly shepherd. He does not treat us as a commodity, balancing profit and risk: he cares for each one of us as if we were the only one.

In the debates Jesus is said to have had in the Temple courts during the week leading up to his arrest, there is a rather puzzling little story about him turning the tables and asking his opponents a tricky question. Referring to the common belief that the Messiah is the "Son of David", he quotes a psalm that refers to the Messiah as "Lord", and says "If David thus calls him Lord, how can he be his son?" (Matt 22:41-46 etc.; Ps 110:1). Jesus elsewhere seems not to have objected to being addressed as "Son of David", and Luke's Gospel represents the angel Gabriel as implying this (Luke 1:32). It could be that Jesus is denying the identification of himself with the Messiah, but this too is uncharacteristic: he was often reticent about being called the Messiah, but he is nowhere said to have categorically denied it. The idea that Jesus was both Messiah and Son of David was a strong belief among the earliest Christians, and so one cannot imagine that the Gospel writers would have made this story up. It is tempting to conclude that at this point, having dealt with a lot of hostile questioning, Jesus was just having a bit of fun with the rabbis by showing how easy it was to ask trick questions! At the same time, behind the apparent trick there could be an important point that is not immediately apparent but needs to be teased out. There is something very characteristic of Jesus in this saying. Rather than making a plain statement, he is saying something cryptic and unexpected in order to prod people into thinking "outside the box".

There are also isolated sayings here and there that seem inconsistent with most people's image of Jesus. What did he mean, for example, by saying to a foreign woman who appealed to him for help, "It is not fair to take the children's food and throw it to the dogs" (Matt 15:26; Mark 7:27)? Why is it that in Luke's Gospel, the one that features the kindness and gentleness of Jesus even more than the others, Jesus suddenly tells the disciples at the last supper that they will now need swords even if they have to sell their cloaks to buy them? And when they point out that they have two swords, what does he mean by saying "It is enough" (Luke 22:35-38)?

And so, even if it were possible to dig back through the accumulated traditions and adaptations of Jesus' sayings and doings and find the actual "Jesus of history", we would probably find an enigmatic character who in some ways would be just as challenging and difficult to grasp as ever. For those who feel the need for certainty this is disconcerting, but if the essence of faith is an ongoing quest, it is appropriate that the one who for Christians is the key to it is one who constantly surprises and puzzles us, one who seems to slip through our fingers whenever we try to grasp him. The character of Jesus himself reminds us that in the spiritual quest we are chasing an elusive God.

Notes

1. George Tyrrell, *Christianity at the Crossroads* (1913), p 44

Epilogue

"To travel hopefully is a better thing than to arrive", said Robert Louis Stevenson[1]. However, if we take this too literally we make it almost a misfortune to arrive. In fact, what does "travel hopefully" mean if we are not hoping to get somewhere?

The same could be said of too much emphasis on spiritual seeking. Is the present-day fashion of using words like "seeking", "quest" and "journey" really a mask for our doubt as to whether or not there is an ultimate truth to be found? Is it perhaps a sign of our unwillingness to make up our minds and commit ourselves to something? There can even be a kind of smugness about it. It seems to be saying: "I'm not one of those boring, unimaginative people who have a fixed set of beliefs. I'm a seeker".

It is, as we have seen, obvious that the faith expressed in the Bible is often a seeking faith. The mystery of God and the future of the universe is so far beyond us that we can never say we have arrived. The concept of seeking is, I believe, essential to genuine spirituality and to an understanding of the Bible. Religion for too long has been perceived as something firm and definite, laid down from the beginning of time, and the Bible has been seen as part of this firm foundation, an "authority" that puts the damper on new, adventurous thinking. Our present-day emphasis on "seeking" is a necessary corrective to that attitude, and it is better to err on the side of uncertainty than on the side of complacency or of intolerant dogmatism.

However, we have to recognize that finding is a valid experience too. The Bible is not only a record of seeking, it is also a celebration of things gained and accomplished, truths discovered, victories won, journeys completed, confident faith. The note of exuberant joy is often expressed in the psalms: "When the LORD restored the fortunes of Zion, we were like

197

those who dream. Then our mouth was filled with laughter, and our tongue with shouts of joy" (Ps 126:1-2). Although there is much anguish and earnest seeking in the Bible, there are times when faith is sure, and the presence of God is experienced as a present reality.

The way in which Jesus talked of the kingdom of God reflects this. At a time when people were speculating about when it would come, his assertion (Luke 17:20-21) was that it was already here: "The kingdom of God is not coming with things that can be observed, nor will they say, 'Look, here it is!' or 'There it is!' For, in fact, the kingdom of God is among you". Another possible translation is "within you".

John's Gospel especially brings out the present reality of the experience of believers as the fulfilment of the promise of Christ's coming. "The hour is coming, and is now here...", as Jesus says to the Samaritan woman (John 4:23). One of the disciples asks why Jesus does not reveal himself to the whole world. This was a question that would have been highly relevant when John's Gospel was written some decades after the time of Jesus and people were asking whether this "return" was ever going to happen. Jesus, according to John, replies that those who love him will find that both the Father and the Son will come and make their home with them (John 14:22-23). For the writer of John's Gospel, "Christ will come again" was a reality already happening. Here, perhaps, is the ultimate paradox of seeking and finding: we look for something, but somehow we find it when we stop looking and realise it has been there all the time.

In most of the Bible the good news has a strong element of *promise* about it. The Letter to the Hebrews talks of the heroes of faith in the Jewish scriptures, describing them all as forward-looking people and saying that "they did not receive what was promised" because God's purpose was that they would not be complete without us. Then it goes on to imply that the complete fulfilment has still not arrived. We have a race set before us, with

Jesus as "the pioneer and the perfecter of our faith": both the starting point and the ultimate goal (Heb 11:1 – 12:2).

The appearance of Jesus in the world is represented as an accomplished event, the fulfilment of everything the prophets dreamed of, and yet at the same it is still a promise of something to come. The Resurrection, rather than being the end of the story, is a new beginning. Matthew's Gospel ends with the words, "I am with you always, to the end of the age". The entire Christian Bible as we now have it ends with the promise of the new heaven and the new earth, and with Jesus saying "Surely I am coming soon", to which the writer, and presumably the readers, respond "Amen. Come, Lord Jesus!" (Rev 22:20).

Christians believe the whole Bible should be interpreted in the light of Jesus as its central character and theme, and so it is appropriate that we find in the Bible the themes both of finality and of promise, of seeking and finding and seeking again. The New Testament writers believed that there is a completeness and finality, and at the same time an openness about the way God is revealed in Jesus. The saying, "I am the way, the truth and the life" (John 14:6) perhaps sums it up very well. Christians are those who believe that, while we are still on a journey of discovery and the ultimate truth is still beyond us, the person of Jesus is the key to the quest: not the end, but the way; not all the answers, but the truth embodied in a person; not a list of rules for living, but the life.

Notes

1. Virginibus Puerisque (Digireads.com edition, 2004, p 85

Suggestions For Further Reading

I offer here a selection of the books that have inspired and stimu-
lated me in the writing of this book and would interest the reader
who wishes to go further into the issues raised.

For a general introduction to reading the Bible I would
recommend:

John Barton, *The Bible: The Basics* (Routledge 2010)

Paula Gooder, *Searching for Meaning: An Introduction to
Interpreting the New Testament* (SPCK 2008). This gives an
overview of all the different kinds of New Testament criticism.

John Holdsworth, *Getting Started with the Bible: A Guide for
Complete Beginners* (Canterbury Press 2007)

John Riches, *The Bible: A Very Short Introduction* (Oxford
University Press 2000)

Keith Ward, *The Word of God: The Bible After Modern Scholarship*
(SPCK 2010)

Probably the most interesting writer about the nature and
authority of the Bible a few decades ago was James Barr. Some
of his books are now out of print, but are well worth reading
if you can find them. They include:

The Bible in the Modern World (SCM 1973)

Old and New in Interpretation (1966, 2nd edition, SCM 1982)

The Scope and Authority of the Bible (1980, re-issued with preface by
John Barton, SCM 2002)

Another very interesting writer of around that time was Dennis E
Nineham, whose books include:

The Use and Abuse of the Bible (Macmillan 1976, Paperback SPCK
1978)

Explorations in Theology 1 (SCM 1977)

In recent years there has been a new wave of books about the
Bible. Among them are those of John Barton:

Ethics and the Old Testament (2nd ed., SCM, 2002)

What is the Bible? (3rd revised edition, SPCK 2009)

People of the Book? The Authority of the Bible in Christianity (3rd revised edition, SPCK 2011)

Several recent books concentrate on the challenge of those parts of the Bible we today find most unacceptable. These include:

Eryl W Davies, *The Immoral Bible: Approaches to Biblical Ethics* (T & T Clark 2010)

Gerd Lüdemann, *The Unholy in Holy scripture: The Dark Side of the Bible* (English translation by John Bowden, SCM 1997)

John Shelby Spong, *The Sins of scripture: Exposing the Bible's Texts of Hate to Reveal the God of Love* (HarperOne 2009)

Adrian Thatcher, *The Savage Text: The Use and Abuse of the Bible* (Wiley-Blackwell 2008)

There are many books that deal with the question of the "Jesus of History". One very good one is:

Marcus J Borg, *Jesus: Uncovering the Life, Teachings, and Relevance of a Religious Revolutionary* (HarperOne 2006)

Gerd Theissen's book, *The Shadow of the Galilean* (SCM 2001) is a fascinating read. It presents the results of "Jesus of history" research in the form of a detective novel. An investigator goes around collecting evidence about Jesus from those who knew him but never actually meeting him in the flesh: the very thing that biblical scholars are doing.

An issue that has to be faced today is that the present generation in the West is largely unfamiliar with the Bible and with the traditional beliefs and culture of the Christian church. Writers concerning themselves with this situation are:

Marcus J Borg: *Reading the Bible Again for the First Time: Taking the Bible Seriously but not Literally* (Harper Collins 2002)

Lloyd Pietersen: *Reading the Bible After Christendom* (Paternoster 2011)

John Shelby Spong, *Re-Claiming the Bible for a Non-Religious World* (HarperOne 2011)

Bart D Ehrman reminds us, often in a provocative way, that there were different forms of Christian belief in the early days of the church, most of which were eventually suppressed and their writings not included in the New Testament. His books include:

Lost scriptures: Books that Did Not Make It into the New Testament (Oxford University Press 2005)

Lost Christianities: The Battles for scripture and the Faiths We Never Knew (Oxford University Press 2005)

Whose Word Is It? The Story Behind Who Changed the New Testament and Why (Continuum 2006)

Jesus, Interrupted: Revealing the Hidden Contradictions in the Bible (and why we don't know about them) (HarperOne 2009)

The impact of archaeology on our view of the history behind the Hebrew scriptures is treated by Israel Finkelstein and Neil Asher Silberman, *The Bible Unearthed: Archaeology's New Vision of Ancient Israel and the Origin of its Sacred Texts* (Touchstone, Simon and Schuster 2002)

Philip R Davies is the best known of a group of scholars rather unfairly labelled "minimalist" who investigate the history behind the Jewish scriptures, concluding that most of the story comes from the community who settled in the land some time after the Babylonian Exile. His books include:

In Search of 'Ancient Israel' (Sheffield Academic Press, 2nd edition 1992)

Memories of Ancient Israel: An Introduction to Biblical History – Ancient and Modern (Westminster John Knox Press 2008)

The Origins of Biblical Israel (Continuum 2009)

A book in similar vein is Thomas L Thompson, *The Bible in History: How Writers Create a Past* (Jonathan Cape 1999)

For a more conservative, but very interesting, view of the Bible I would recommend N T Wright, *Scripture and the Authority of God* (SPCK 2005)

Probably the most popular and stimulating thinker about the

Bible today is Walter Brueggemann. He is a prolific writer, focussing mainly on the Hebrew scriptures. He points out that the prophets were essentially poets, and that their main theme was the presenting of an alternative to the totalitarian tendencies of "empire". He relates this to life in the United States (and Western culture generally) today. His books include:

The Prophetic Imagination (2nd Edition, Fortress Press 2001)

The Bible Makes Sense (Westminster John Knox Press 2001)

Redescribing Reality: What we do when we read the Bible (SCM 2009)

An Unsettling God: The Heart of the Hebrew Bible (Fortress Press 2009)

Out of Babylon (Abingdon Press 2010)

(With Carolyn J Sharpe) *Disruptive Grace: Reflections on God, Scripture and the Church* (Fortress 2011)

CHRISTIAN
ALTERNATIVE

Throughout the two thousand years of Christian tradition there
have been, and still are, groups and individuals that exist in the
margins and upon the edge of faith. But in Christianity's
contrapuntal history it has often been these outcasts and
pioneers that have forged contemporary orthodoxy out of
former radicalism as belief evolves to engage with and
encompass the ever-changing social and scientific realities. Real
faith lies not in the comfortable certainties of the Orthodox, but
somewhere in a half-glimpsed hinterland on the dirt track to
Emmaus, where the Death of God meets the Resurrection, where
the supernatural Christ meets the historical Jesus, and where the
revolution liberates both the oppressed and the oppressors.

Welcome to Christian Alternative... a space at the edge where
the light shines through.